THE GREAT GATSBY

F. Scott Fitzgerald

AUTHORED by Jeremy Ross
UPDATED AND REVISED by Rachel Nolan

COVER DESIGN by Table XI Partners LLC
COVER PHOTO by Olivia Verma and © 2005 GradeSaver, LLC

BOOK DESIGN by Table XI Partners LLC

Published by GradeSaver LLC, www.gradesaver.com

First published in the United States of America by GradeSaver LLC. 2000

GRADESAVER, the GradeSaver logo and the phrase "Getting you the grade
since 1999" are registered trademarks of GradeSaver, LLC

ISBN 978-1-60259-034-2

Printed in the United States of America

For other products and additional information please visit
http://www.gradesaver.com

Table of Contents

Biography of F. Scott Fitzgerald (1896–1940)..1

About The Great Gatsby..5

Character List...7

Major Themes..11

Glossary of Terms...15

Short Summary..17

Summary and Analysis of Chapter 1..21
    Chapter One...21
    Analysis..21

Summary and Analysis of Chapter 2..23
    Chapter Two..23
    Analysis..23

Summary and Analysis of Chapter 3..25
    Chapter Three..25
    Analysis..26

Summary and Analysis of Chapter 4..27
    Chapter Four..27
    Analysis..28

Summary and Analysis of Chapter 5..31
    Chapter Five..31
    Analysis..32

Summary and Analysis of Chapter 6..35
    Chapter Six..35
    Analysis..36

Summary and Analysis of Chapter 7..39
    Chapter Seven...39
    Analysis..40

Summary and Analysis of Chapter 8..43
    Chapter Eight..43
    Analysis..44

Table of Contents

Summary and Analysis of Chapter 9..45

    Chapter Nine..45

    Analysis..46

Suggested Essay Questions...47

Fitzgerald and the Lost Generation...49

Author of ClassicNote and Sources..51

Essay: Foreshadowing Destiny...53

Essay: The Eulogy of a Dream...57

Quiz 1...61

Quiz 1 Answer Key...67

Quiz 2...69

Quiz 2 Answer Key...75

Quiz 3...77

Quiz 3 Answer Key...83

Quiz 4...85

Quiz 4 Answer Key...91

Biography of F. Scott Fitzgerald (1896–1940)

Francis Scott Key Fitzgerald was a Jazz Age novelist and short story writer who is considered to be among the greatest twentieth–century American writers. Born on September 24, 1896, he was the only son of an aristocratic father and a provincial, working–class mother. He was the product of two divergent traditions: while his father's family included the author of "The Star–Spangled Banner" (after whom Fitzgerald was named), his mother's family was, in Fitzgerald's own words, "straight 1850 potato–famine Irish." As a result of this contrast, he was exceedingly ambivalent toward the notion of the American dream: for him, it was at once vulgar and dazzlingly promising.

Like the central character of The Great Gatsby, Fitzgerald had an intensely romantic imagination; he once called it "a heightened sensitivity to the promises of life." The events of Fitzgerald's own life can be seen as a struggle to realize those promises.

He attended both St. Paul Academy (1908–10) and Newman School (1911–13), where his intensity and outsized enthusiasm made him unpopular with the other students. Later, at Princeton University, he came close to the brilliant success of which he dreamed. He became part of the influential Triangle Club, a dramatic organization whose members were taken from the cream of society. He also became a prominent figure in the literary life of the university and made lifelong friendships with Edmund Wilson and John Peale Bishop. Despite these social coups, Fitzgerald struggled academically, and he eventually flunked out of Princeton. In November 1917, he joined the army.

While stationed at Camp Sheridan (near Montgomery, Alabama), he met Zelda Sayre, the daughter of an Alabama Supreme Court judge, and the two fell deeply in love. Fitzgerald needed to improve his dismal financial circumstances, however, before he and Zelda could marry. At the first opportunity, he left for New York, determined to make his fortune in the great city. Instead, he was forced to take a menial advertising job at $90 per month. Zelda broke their engagement, and Fitzgerald retreated to St. Paul, Minnesota. There, he rewrote a novel that he had begun at Princeton. In the spring of 1920 the novel, *This Side of Paradise*, was published.

Though today's readers might find its ideas dated, *This Side of Paradise* was a revelation to Fitzgerald's contemporaries. It was regarded as a rare glimpse into the morality and immorality of America's youth, and it made Fitzgerald famous. Suddenly, the author could publish not only in prestigious literary magazines such as *Scribner's* but also high–paying, popular publications including *The Saturday Evening Post*.

Flush with his new wealth and fame, Fitzgerald finally married Zelda. The celebrated columnist Ring Lardner christened them "the prince and princess of their generation." Though the Fitzgeralds reveled in their notoriety, they also found it frightening, a fact which is perhaps represented in the ending of Fitzgerald's second novel. This novel, *The Beautiful and Damned,* was published two years later, and tells the story of a handsome young man and his beautiful wife, who gradually deteriorate into careworn middle age while they wait for the young man to inherit a large fortune. In a predictable ironic twist, they only receive their inheritance when it is too late.

To escape this grim fate, the Fitzgeralds (together with their daughter, Frances, who was born in 1921) moved in 1924 to the Riviera, where they became part of a group of wealthy American expatriates whose style was largely determined by Gerald and Sara Murphy. Fitzgerald described this society in his last completed novel, *Tender is the Night,* and modeled its hero on Gerald Murphy. Meanwhile, Fitzgerald's reputation as a heavy drinker tarnished his reputation in the literary world; he was viewed as an irresponsible writer despite his painstaking revisions numerous drafts of his work.

Shortly after their relocation to France, Fitzgerald completed his most famous and respected novel, *The Great Gatsby* (1925). Fitzgerald's own divided nature can be seen in the contrast between the novel's hero, Jay Gatsby, and its narrator, Nick Carraway. The former represents the naive Midwesterner dazzled by the possibilities of the American dream; the latter represents the compassionate Princeton gentleman who cannot help but regard that dream with suspicion. The Great Gatsby may be described as the most profoundly American novel of its time; Fitzgerald connects Gatsby's dream, his "Platonic conception of himself," with the aspirations of the founders of America.

A year later, Fitzgerald published a collection of short stories, *All the Sad Young Men.* This book marks the end of the most productive period of Fitzgerald's life; the next decade was full of chaos and misery. Fitzgerald began to drink excessively, and Zelda began a slow descent into madness. In 1930, she suffered her first mental breakdown. Her second breakdown, from which she never fully recovered, came in 1932.

Throughout the 1930s the Fitzgeralds fought an ultimately unsuccessful battle to save their marriage. This struggle was tremendously debilitating for Fitzgerald; he later said that he "left [his] capacity for hoping on the little roads that led to Zelda's sanitarium." He did not finish his next novel, *Tender is the Night,* until 1934. It is the story of a psychiatrist who marries one of his patients, and, as she slowly recovers, she exhausts his vitality until he is "a man used up." This book, the last that Fitzgerald ever completed, was considered technically faulty and was commercially unsuccessful. It has since gained a reputation, however, as Fitzgerald's most moving work.

Crushed by the failure of *Tender is the Night* and his despair over Zelda, Fitzgerald became an incurable alcoholic. In 1937, however, he managed to acquire work as a script–writer in Hollywood. There he met and fell in love with Sheilah Graham, a famous Hollywood gossip columnist. For the rest of his life, though he frequently had drunken spells in which he became bitter and violent, Fitzgerald lived quietly with Ms. Graham. Occasionally he went east to visit Zelda or his daughter Frances, who entered Vassar College in 1938.

In October 1939, Fitzgerald began a novel about Hollywood titled *The Last Tycoon*. The career of its hero, Monroe Stahr, is based on that of the renowned Hollywood producer Irving Thalberg. On December 21, 1940, Fitzgerald suffered a fatal heart attack, leaving the novel unfinished. Even in its half–completed state, *The Last Tycoon* is considered the equal of the rest of Fitzgerald's work for its intensity.

Biography of F. Scott Fitzgerald (1896–1940)

About The Great Gatsby

The Great Gatsby, published in 1925, is widely considered to be F. Scott Fitzergerald's greatest novel. It is also considered a seminal work on the fallibility of the American dream. It focuses on a young man, Jay Gatsby, who, after falling in love with a woman from the social elite, makes a lot of money in an effort to win her love. She marries a man from her own social strata and he dies disillusioned with the concept of a self–made man. Fitzgerald seems to argue that the possibility of social mobility in America is an illusion, and that the social hierarchies of the "New World" are just as rigid as those of Europe.

The novel is also famous as a description of the "Jazz Age," a phrase which Fitzgerald himself coined. After the shock of moving from a policy of isolationism to involvement in World War I, America prospered in what are termed the "Roaring Twenties." The Eighteenth Amendment to the American Constitution, passed in 1919, prohibited the sale and consumption of alcohol in America. "Prohibition" made millionaires out of bootleggers like Gatsby and owners of underground salons, called "speakeasies." Fitzgerald glamorizes the noveau riche of this period to a certain extent in his Jazz Age novel. He describes their beautiful clothing and lavish parties with great attention to detail and wonderful use of color. However, the author was uncomfortable with the excesses of the period, and his novel sounds many warning notes against excessive love of money and material success.

Fitzgerald's The Great Gatsby was not a great success during his lifetime, but became a smash hit after his death, especially after World War II. It has since become a staple of the canon of American literature, and is taught at many high schools and universities across the country and the world. Four films, an opera, and a play have been made from the text.

Character List

Jay Gatsby (James Gatz)

Gatsby is, of course, both the novel's title character and its protagonist. Gatsby is a mysterious, fantastically wealthy young man. Every Saturday, his garish Gothic mansion in West Egg serves as the site of extravagant parties. Later in the novel, we learn that his real name is James Gatz; he was born in North Dakota to an impoverished farming family. While serving in the Army in World War I, Gatsby met Daisy Fay (now Daisy Buchanan) and fell passionately in love with her. He worked briefly for a millionaire, and became acquainted with the people and customs of high society. This, coupled with his love of Daisy, inspired Gatsby to devote his life to the acquisition of wealth.

Nick Carraway

The novel's narrator, Nick Carraway comes from a well–to–do Minnesota family. He travels to New York to learn the bond business; there, he becomes involved with both Gatsby and the Buchanans. Though he is honest, responsible, and fair–minded, Nick does share some of the flaws of the East Egg milieu. However, of all the novel's characters, he is the only one to recognize Gatsby's "greatness," - revealing himself as a young man of unusual sensitivity.

Daisy Buchanan

Daisy is Nick's cousin, Tom's wife, and the woman that Gatsby loves. She had promised to wait for Jay Gatsby until the end of the war, but after meeting Tom Buchanan and comparing his extreme wealth to Gatsby's poverty, she broke her promise. Daisy uses her frailty as an excuse for her extreme immaturity.

Tom Buchanan

A brutal, hulking man, Tom Buchanan is a former Yale football player who, like Daisy, comes from an immensely wealthy Midwestern family. His racism and sexism are symptomatic of his deep insecurity about his elevated social position. Tom is a vicious bully, physically menacing both his wife and his mistress. He is a thoroughgoing hypocrite as well: though he condemns his wife for her infidelity, he has no qualms about carrying on an affair himself.

Jordan Baker

Daisy's longtime friend, Jordan Baker is a professional golfer who cheated in order to win her first tournament. Jordan is extremely cynical, with a masculine, icy demeanor that Nick initially finds compelling. The two become briefly involved, but Jordan rejects him on the grounds that he is as corrupt and decadent as she is.

Myrtle Wilson

An earthy, vital, and voluptuous woman, Myrtle is desperate to improve her life. She shares a loveless marriage with George Wilson, a man who runs a shabby garage. She has been having a long-term affair with Tom Buchanan, and is very jealous of his wife, Daisy. After a fight with her husband, she runs out into the street and is hit and killed by Gatsby's car.

George B. Wilson

George is a listless, impoverished man whose only passion is his love for his wife, Myrtle. He is devastated by Myrtle's affair with Tom. After her death, the magnitude of his grief drives Wilson to murder Jay Gatsby before committing suicide himself.

Henry Gatz

Gatsby's father; his son's help is the only thing that saves him from poverty. Gatz tells Nick about his son's extravagant plans and dreams of self-improvement.

Meyer Wolfsheim

A notorious underworld figure, Wolfsheim is a business associate of Gatsby. He is deeply involved in organized crime, and even claims credit for fixing the 1919 World Series. His character, like Fitzgerald's view of the Roaring Twenties as a whole, is a curious mix of barbarism and refinement (his cuff links are made from human molars). After Gatsby's murder, however, Wolfsheim is one of the only people to express his grief or condolences; in contrast, the socially superior Buchanans fail to attend Gatsby's funeral.

Dan Cody

Dan is a somewhat coarse man who became immensely wealthy during the Gold Rush. He mentored Gatsby was he was a young man and gave him a taste of elite society. Though he left Gatsby a sum of money after his death, it was later seized by his ex-wife.

Michaelis

Wilson's neighbor; he attempts to console Wilson after Myrtle's death.

Catherine

Myrtle Wilson's sister. Tom, Myrtle, and Nick visit her and her neighbors, the McKees, in New York City.

The McKees

Catherine's neighbors. The couple is shallow and gossipy and concern themselves only with status and fashion.

Ewing Klipspringer

A shiftless freeloader who almost lives at Gatsby's mansion. Though he takes advantage of Gatsby's wealth and generosity, Klipspringer fails to attend his funeral.

Owl Eyes

An eccentric, bespectacled man whom Nick meets at one of Gatsby's parties. He is one of the few people to attend Gatsby's funeral.

Major Themes

Honesty

Honesty is does not seem to determine which characters are sympathetic and which are not in this novel in quite the same way that it does in others. Nick is able to admire Gatsby despite his knowledge of the man's illegal dealings and bootlegging. Ironically, it is the corrupt Daisy who takes pause at Gatsby's sordid past. Her indignation at his "dishonesty," however, is less moral than class–based. Her sense of why Gatsby should not behave in an immoral manner is based on what she expects from members of her milieu, rather than what she believes to be intrinsically right. The standards for honesty and morality seem to be dependent on class and gender in this novel. Tom finds his wife's infidelity intolerable, however, he does not hesitate to lie to her about his own affair.

Decay

Decay is a word that constantly comes up in The Great Gatsby, which is appropriate in a novel which centers around the death of the American Dream. Decay is most evident in the so–called "valley of ashes." With great virtuosity, Fitzgerald describes a barren wasteland which probably has little to do with the New York landscape and instead serves to comment on the downfall of American society. It seems that the American dream has been perverted, reversed. Gatsby lives in West Egg and Daisy in East Egg; therefore, Gatsby looks East with yearning, rather than West, the traditional direction of American frontier ambitions. Fitzgerald portrays the chauvinistic and racist Tom in a very negative light, clearly scoffing at his apocalyptic vision of the races intermarrying. Fitzgerald's implication seems to be that society has already decayed enough and requires no new twist.

Gender Roles

In some respects, Fitzgerald writes about gender roles in a quite conservative manner. In his novel, men work to earn money for the maintenance of the women. Men are dominant over women, especially in the case of Tom, who asserts his physical strength to subdue them. The only hint of a role reversal is in the pair of Nick and Jordan. Jordan's androgynous name and cool, collected style masculinize her more than any other female character. However, in the end, Nick does exert his dominance over her by ending the relationship. The women in the novel are an interesting group, because they do not divide into the traditional groups of Mary Magdalene and Madonna figures, instead, none of them are pure. Myrtle is the most obviously sensual, but the fact that Jordan and Daisy wear white dresses only highlights their corruption.

Violence

Violence is a key theme in The Great Gatsby, and is most embodied by the character of Tom. An ex–football player, he uses his immense physical strength to intimidate those around him. When Myrtle taunts him with his wife's name, he strikes her across the face. The other source of violence in the novel besides Tom are cars. A new commodity at the time that The Great Gatsby was published, Fitzgerald uses cars to symbolize the dangers of modernity and the dangers of wealth. The climax of the novel, the accident that kills Myrtle, is foreshadowed by the conversation between Nick and Jordan about how bad driving can cause explosive violence. The end of the novel, of course, consists of violence against Gatsby. The choice of handgun as a weapon suggests Gatsby's shady past, but it is symbolic that it is his love affair, not his business life, that kills Gatsby in the end.

Class

Class is an unusual theme for an American novel. It is more common to find references to it in European, especially British novels. However, the societies of East and West Egg are deeply divided by the difference between the noveau riche and the older moneyed families. Gatsby is aware of the existence of a class structure in America, because a true meritocracy would put him in touch with some of the finest people, but, as things stand, he is held at arm's length. Gatsby tries desperately to fake status, even buying British shirts and claiming to have attended Oxford in an attempt to justify his position in society. Ultimately, however, it is a class gulf that seperates Gatsby and Daisy, and cements the latter in her relationship to her husbad, who is from the same class as she is.

Religion

It is interesting that Fitzgerald chooses to use some religious tropes in a novel that focuses on the American Dream, a concept which leaves no room for religion save for the doctrine of individualism. The most obvious is the image of the "valley of ashes," which exemplifies America's moral state during the "Roaring Twenties." This wasteland is presided over by the empty eyes of an advertisement. Fitzgerald strongly implies that these are the eyes of God. This equation of religion with advertising and material gain are made even more terrifying by the fact that the eyes see nothing and can help no one (for example, this "God" can do nothing to prevent Myrtle or Gatsby's deaths).

World War I

Because The Great Gatsby is set in the Roaring Twenties, the topic of the Great War is unavoidable. The war was crucial to Gatsby's development, providing a brief period of social mobility which, Fitzgerald claims, quickly closed after the war. Gatsby only came into contact with a classy young debutante like Daisy as a result of the fact that he was a soldier and that no one could vouch for whether he was upper–class or not. The war provided him with further opportunities to see the world, and make some money in the service of a millionaire. Gatsby's opportunities closed up after the end of the war, however, when he found upon returning to America that the social structure there was every bit as rigid as it was in Europe. Unable to convince anyone that he is truly upper–class (although his participation in the war gave him some leeway about lying), Gatsby finds himself unable to break into East Egg society.

Glossary of Terms

corpulent

having a large, cumbersome body

denizen

inhabitant

dilatory

procrastinatory

ectoplasm

a gel–like material which supposedly helps to summon spirits

euphemism

substitution of an inoffensive phrase or word for an offensive one

fortuitous

occurring by chance; lucky; serendipitous

fractious

unruly; quarrelsome; irritable

garrulous

pointlessly wordy; over–talkative

malevolence

intense ill will

meritricious

tawdry; gaudy

peremptory

admitting no argument; characterized by arrogant self–assurance

portentious

self–consciously weighty; pompous

prodigality

lavishness; reckless luxury

provincial

limited; narrow; unsophisticated

punctilious

characterized by extreme attention to detail

redolent

aromatic; scented; suggestive of

strident

commanding attention with volume or obtrusiveness

supercilious

contemptuous

turgid

swollen; bombastic in style

Glossary of Terms

Short Summary

While The Great Gatsby is a highly specific portrait of American society during the Roaring Twenties, its story is also one that has been told hundreds of times, and is perhaps as old as America itself: a man claws his way from rags to riches, only to find that his wealth cannot afford him the privileges enjoyed by those born into the upper class. The central character is Jay Gatsby, a wealthy New Yorker of indeterminate occupation. Gatsby is primarily known for the lavish parties he throws each weekend at his ostentatious Gothic mansion in West Egg. He is suspected of being involved in illegal bootlegging and other underworld activities.

The narrator, Nick Carraway, is Gatsby's neighbor in West Egg. Nick is a young man from a prominent Midwestern family. Educated at Yale, he has come to New York to enter the bond business. In some sense, the novel is Nick's memoir, his unique view of the events of the summer of 1922; as such, his impressions and observations necessarily color the narrative as a whole. For the most part, he plays only a peripheral role in the events of the novel; he prefers to remain a passive observer.

Upon arriving in New York, Nick visits his cousin, Daisy Buchanan, and her husband, Tom. The Buchanans live in the posh Long Island district of East Egg; Nick, like Gatsby, resides in nearby West Egg, a less fashionable area looked down upon by those who live in East Egg. West Egg is home to the nouveau riche, people who lack established social connections, and who tend to vulgarly flaunt their wealth. Like Nick, Tom Buchanan graduated from Yale, and comes from a privileged Midwestern family. Tom is a former football player, a brutal bully obsessed with the preservation of class boundaries. Daisy, by contrast, is an almost ghostlike young woman who affects an air of sophisticated boredom. At the Buchanans's, Nick meets Jordan Baker, a beautiful young woman with a cold, cynical manner. The two later become romantically involved.

Jordan tells Nick that Tom has been having an affair with Myrtle Wilson, a woman who lives in the valley of ashes, - an industrial wasteland outside of New York City. After visiting Tom and Daisy, Nick goes home to West Egg; there, he sees Gatsby gazing at a mysterious green light across the bay. Gatsby stretches his arms out toward the light, as though to catch and hold it.

Tom Buchanan takes Nick into New York, and on the way they stop at the garage owned by George Wilson. Wilson is the husband of Myrtle, with whom Tom has been having an affair. Tom tells Myrtle to join them later in the city. Nearby, on an enormous billboard, a pair of bespectacled blue eyes stares down at the barren landscape. These eyes once served as an advertisement; now, they brood over all that occurs in the valley of ashes.

In the city, Tom takes Nick and Myrtle to the apartment in Morningside Heights at which he maintains his affair. There, they have a lurid party with Myrtle's sister,

Catherine, and an abrasive couple named McKee. They gossip about Gatsby; Catherine says that he is somehow related to Kaiser Wilhelm, the much–despised ruler of Germany during World War I. The more she drinks, the more aggressive Myrtle becomes; she begins taunting Tom about Daisy, and he reacts by breaking her nose. The party, unsurprisingly, comes to an abrupt end.

Nick Carraway attends a party at Gatsby's mansion, where he runs into Jordan Baker. At the party, few of the attendees know Gatsby; even fewer were formally invited. Before the party, Nick himself had never met Gatsby: he is a strikingly handsome, slightly dandified young man who affects an English accent. Gatsby asks to speak to Jordan Baker alone; after talking with Gatsby for quite a long time, she tells Nick that she has learned some remarkable news. She cannot yet share it with him, however.

Some time later, Gatsby visits Nick's home and invites him to lunch. At this point in the novel, Gatsby's origins are unclear. He claims to come from a wealthy San Francisco family, and says that he was educated at Oxford after serving in the Great War (during which he received a number of decorations). At lunch, Gatsby introduces Nick to his business associate, Meyer Wolfsheim. Wolfhsheim is a notorious criminal; many believe that he is responsible for fixing the 1919 World Series.

Gatsby mysteriously avoids the Buchanans. Later, Jordan Baker explains the reason for Gatsby's anxiety: he had been in love with Daisy Buchanan when they met in Louisville before the war. Jordan subtly intimates that he is still in love with her, and she with him.

Gatsby asks Nick to arrange a meeting between himself and Daisy. Gatsby has meticulously planned their meeting: he gives Daisy a carefully rehearsed tour of his mansion, and is desperate to exhibit his wealth and possessions. Gatsby is wooden and mannered during this initial meeting; his dearest dreams have been of this moment, and so the actual reunion is bound to disappoint. Despite this, the love between Gatsby and Daisy is revived, and the two begin an affair.

Eventually, Nick learns the true story of Gatsby's past. He was born James Gatz in North Dakota, but had his name legally changed at the age of seventeen. The gold baron Dan Cody served as Gatsby's mentor until his death. Though Gatsby inherited nothing of Cody's fortune, it was from him that Gatsby was first introduced to world of wealth, power, and privilege.

While out horseback riding, Tom Buchanan happens upon Gatsby's mansion. There he meets both Nick and Gatsby, to whom he takes an immediate dislike. To Tom, Gatsby is part of the "new rich," and thus poses a danger to the old order that Tom holds dear. Despite this, he accompanies Daisy to Gatsby's next party; there, he is exceedingly rude and condescending toward Gatsby. Nick realizes that Gatsby wants Daisy to renounce her husband and her marriage; in this way, they can recover the years they have lost since they first parted. Gatsby's great flaw is that his great love of Daisy is a kind of worship, and that he fails to see her flaws. He believes that he can undo the past, and forgets that Daisy's essentially small–minded and cowardly nature was what initially caused their separation.

After his reunion with Daisy, Gatsby ceases to throw his elaborate parties. The only reason he threw such parties was the chance that Daisy (or someone who knew her) might attend. Daisy invites Gatsby, Nick and Jordan to lunch at her house. In an attempt to make Tom jealous, and to exact revenge for his affair, Daisy is highly indiscreet about her relationship with Gatsby. She even tells Gatsby that she loves him while Tom is in earshot.

Although Tom is himself having an affair, he is furious at the thought that his wife could be unfaithful to him. He forces the group to drive into the city: there, in a suite at the Plaza Hotel, Tom and Gatsby have a bitter confrontation. Tom denounces Gatsby for his low birth, and reveals to Daisy that Gatsby's fortune has been made through illegal activities. Daisy's real allegiance is to Tom: when Gatsby begs her to say that she does not love her husband, she refuses him. Tom permits Gatsby to drive Daisy back to East Egg; in this way, he displays his contempt for Gatsby, as well as his faith in his wife's complete subjection.

On the trip back to East Egg, Gatsby allows Daisy to drive in order to calm her ragged nerves. Passing Wilson's garage, Daisy swerves to avoid another car and ends up hitting Myrtle; she is killed instantly. Nick advises Gatsby to leave town until the situation calms. Gatsby, however, refuses to leave: he remains in order to ensure that Daisy is safe. George Wilson, driven nearly mad by the death of his wife, is desperate to find her killer. Tom Buchanan tells him that Gatsby was the driver of the fatal car. Wilson, who has decided that the driver of the car must also have been Myrtle's lover, shoots Gatsby before committing suicide himself.

After the murder, the Buchanans leave town to distance themselves from the violence for which they are responsible. Nick is left to organize Gatsby's funeral, but finds that few people cared for Gatsby. Only Meyer Wolfsheim shows a modicum of grief, and few people attend the funeral. Nick seeks out Gatsby's father, Henry Gatz, and brings him to New York for the funeral. From Henry, Nick learns the full scope of Gatsby's visions of greatness and his dreams of self–improvement.

Thoroughly disgusted with life in New York, Nick decides to return to the Midwest. Before his departure, Nick sees Tom Buchanan once more. Tom tries to elicit Nick's sympathy; he believes that all of his actions were thoroughly justified, and he wants Nick to agree.

Nick muses that Gatsby, alone among the people of his acquaintance, strove to transform his dreams into reality; it is this that makes him "great." Nick also believes, however, that the time for such grand aspirations is over: greed and dishonesty have irrevocably corrupted both the American Dream and the dreams of individual Americans.

Summary and Analysis of Chapter 1

Chapter One

The narrator, Nick Carraway, begins the novel by commenting on himself: he says that he is very tolerant, and has a tendency to reserve judgment. Carraway comes from a prominent Midwestern family and graduated from Yale; therefore, he fears to be misunderstood by those who have not enjoyed the same advantages. He attempts to understand people on their own terms, rather than holding them up to his own personal standards.

Nick fought in World War I; after the war, he went through a period of restlessness. He eventually decided to go east, to New York City, in order to learn the bond business. At the novel's outset, in the summer of 1922, Carraway has just arrived in New York and is living in a part of Long Island known as West Egg. West Egg is home to the nouveau riche (those who have recently made money and lack an established social position), while neighboring East Egg is home to the insular, narrow–minded denizens of the old aristocracy. Nick's house is next door to Gatsby's enormous, vulgar Gothic mansion.

One night, he attends a dinner party in East Egg; the party is given by Tom Buchanan and his wife, Daisy. Daisy is Nick's cousin, while Tom was Nick's classmate at Yale. Tom comes from a wealthy, established family, and was a much–feared football player while at Yale. A friend of Daisy's is also in attendance. This woman, whose name is Jordan Baker, makes her living as a professional golfer. She has a frigid, boyish beauty and affects an air of extreme boredom.

Tom dominates the conversation at dinner; he wishes to propound ideas he has found in a book entitled "The Rise of the Colored Empires." This book espouses racist and white supremacist ideas, to which Tom wholeheartedly subscribes. When Tom abruptly leaves to take a phone call, Daisy declares that she has become terribly cynical and sophisticated since she and Nick last met. Her claims ring false, however - particularly when contrasted with the genuine cynicism of Jordan Baker, who languidly informs Nick that Tom's phone call is from his lover in New York. After his awkward visit with the Buchanans, Carraway goes home to West Egg. There, he sees a handsome young man, Jay Gatsby, standing on his wide lawn, with his arms stretched out to the sea. He appears to be reaching for a faraway green light, which may mark the end of a dock.

Analysis

Fitzgerald establishes Nick Carraway as an impartial narrator; he is not, however, a passive one. Although he is inclined to reserve judgment, he is not entirely forgiving. From the novel's opening paragraph onward, this will continue create tension in Nick's narrative. Despite the fact that Gatsby represents all that Nick holds in contempt, Nick cannot help but admire him. The first paragraphs of the book foreshadow the novel's main themes: the reader realizes that Gatsby presented, and still presents, a challenge to the way in which Nick is accustomed to thinking about the world. It is clear from the story's opening moments that Gatsby will not be what he initially appears: despite the vulgarity of his mansion, Nick describes Gatsby's personality as "gorgeous."

The novel's characters are obsessed by class and privilege. Though Nick, like the Buchanans, comes from an elite background, the couple's relationship to their social position is entirely distinct to the narrator's. Tom Buchanan vulgarly exploits his status: he is grotesque, completely lacking redeeming features. His wife describes him as a "big, hulking physical specimen," and he seems to use his size only to dominate others. He has a trace of "paternal contempt" that instantly inspires hatred.

Daisy Buchanan stands in stark contrast to her husband. She is frail and diminutive, and actually labors at being shallow. she laughs at every opportunity. Daisy is utterly transparent, feebly affecting an air of worldliness and cynicism. Though she breezily remarks that everything is in decline, she does so only in order to seem to agree with her husband. She and Jordan are dressed in white when Nick arrives, and she mentions that they spent a "white girl–hood" together; the ostensible purity of Daisy and Jordan stands in ironic contrast to their actual decadence and corruption.

The first appearance of Gatsby has a religious solemnity, and Gatsby himself seems almost godlike: Nick speculates that Gatsby has "come out to determine what share of our local heavens [was his]." He is utterly alone, a solitary figure in a posture of mysterious worship. When the reader first sees Gatsby, he is reaching toward the green light - something that, by definition, he cannot grasp. In this scene, Fitzgerald wholly sacrifices realism in favor of drama and symbol: the green light stands for the as–yet–nameless object for which Gatsby is hopelessly striving.

Summary and Analysis of Chapter 1

Summary and Analysis of Chapter 2

Chapter Two

The second chapter begins with a description of the valley of ashes, a dismal, barren wasteland halfway between West Egg and New York. A pair of enormous eyes broods over the valley from a large, decaying billboard. These are the eyes of Dr. T.J. Eckleburg, an optometrist whose practice has long since ended.

Tom Buchanan takes Nick to George Wilson's garage, which lies at the edge of the valley of ashes. Wilson's wife, Myrtle, is the woman with whom Tom has been having an affair. Tom forces both Myrtle and Nick to accompany him to the city. There, in the flat in which Tom maintains his affair, they have a shrill, vulgar party with Myrtle's sister, Catherine, and a repulsive couple named McKee. The group gossips about Jay Gatsby: Catherine claims that he is somehow related to Kaiser Wilhelm, the much–despised ruler of Germany during World War I. The group becomes exceedingly drunk; as a result, Myrtle begins to grow garrulous and harsh. Shortly after Tom gives her a puppy as a gift, Myrtle begins chanting Daisy's name to irritate Tom. Tom tells her that she has no right to say Daisy's name; she continues taunting him, and he responds by breaking Myrtle's nose.

Analysis

The road from West Egg to New York City exemplifies decay. It is a "valley of ashes," a place of uninterrupted desolation. The eyes of Doctor T.J. Eckleburg are an indelibly grotesque image: these are eyes unattached to any face or body, gazing out over a hellish wasteland. Fitzgerald's description of the drawbridge and passing barges makes an allusion to the River Styx, a mythological river which one crosses to enter the realm of the dead. The eyes of Dr. T.J. Eckleburg seem to be a monstrous parody of the eyes of God: they watch, but they do not see; they are heartless, and entirely unknowing. Like the scene in which Gatsby reaches for the green light, high symbolism is given priority over the demands of realism: the reader is presented with an implausible, but highly effective image of two detached eyes looking out over dust and ashes.

The novel's only non–wealthy characters live in the valley of ashes; it is the grim underside to the hedonism of the Eggs, and of New York City. George Wilson, Myrtle's dejected husband, seems almost made of ashes: "ashen dust" coats his clothes and his hair. Fitzgerald represents poverty as lying beneath wealth and providing the wealthy with a dumping ground. It is what the wealthy wish to avoid seeing at all costs.

In comparison to Daisy Buchanan, Myrtle Wilson is sensuous and vital. While Daisy wears pale white, Myrtle dresses in saturated colors and her mouth is a deep red. While Daisy is affected and insubstantial, Myrtle Wilson is straightforward, fleshy, almost coarse. Fitzgerald presents her fleshy breasts and large hips as a sign of her robust femininity.

At Tom's party, the characters engage in vulgar, boorish behavior: Myrtle Wilson reads tabloids; she and her sister gossip viciously about Gatsby and each other; Mr. McKee does not say that he is an artist, but instead claims to be in the "artistic game."

Clothing plays an important role in the development of character, and is reflective of both a character's mood and his or her personality. This device emphasizes the characters' superficiality. When Myrtle changes into a cream–colored dress, she loses some of her vitality. Like Daisy, she becomes more artificial; her laughter, gestures, and speech become violently affected.

This chapter explores a world that has collapsed into decadence: Fitzgerald's society is a society in decay. The only rationale that Myrtle gives for her affair with Tom is: "You can't live forever." Nick Carraway remains both "within and without" this world: though he is repulsed by the party's vulgarity, he is too fascinated to compel himself to leave. It becomes patently clear in this chapter that Tom is both a bully and a hypocrite: he carries on a highly public affair, but feels compelled to beat his mistress in order to keep her in her place. The fact that Tom feels no guilt about his violence toward Myrtle (indeed, he seems incapable of feeling guilt at all) becomes pivotal in later chapters.

Summary and Analysis of Chapter 2

Summary and Analysis of Chapter 3

Chapter Three

This chapter begins with Nick's description of Gatsby's Saturday night parties: they have become legendary in New York for their opulence and hedonism. These parties are obscenely lavish. The guests marvel at Gatsby's Rolls–Royce, his enormous swimming pool, the live musicians he engages weekly, the sumptuous food that he provides for hundreds of people, and, perhaps most importantly, the unlimited liquor he generously supplies. Nick is eventually invited to one of these parties, but not by Gatsby himself; instead, Gatsby's chauffeur brings an invitation to Nick's door.

Gatsby's mansion is packed with revelers when Nick arrives. Very few of them seem to be invited guests, and even fewer have met Gatsby face to face. It is a very mixed crowd: East Eggers rub elbows with West Eggers, and people from New York high society meet those from "the wrong side of the tracks." Nick runs into Jordan Baker, who is even more casually bitter than usual because she has recently lost a golf tournament. All around them, people gossip about their mysterious host. They speculate that he once killed a man in cold blood or that he was a spy for Germany during World War I.

Jordan and Nick go looking for Gatsby in his mansion; instead, they find a grotesque little man in enormous eyeglasses (Nick calls him "Owl Eyes") skimming through the books in Gatsby's library. Both Owl Eyes and Jordan initially think that the books are false, designed only to give the appearance of a library; both are surprised to find that the books are real.

Outside, in the garden, Nick strikes up a conversation with a handsome, youthful man who looks familiar to him; it turns out that they served in the same division during the war. This man is the mysterious Gatsby. Gatsby has an affected English accent and a highly formal way of speaking. He stands aloof from his guests, watching the party rather than taking part in it. Gatsby leaves to take a phone call; later, he sends his butler to ask Jordan Baker if he may speak with her privately. When she finishes talking to Gatsby, she tells Nick that she has heard some "remarkable" news.

At about two in the morning, Nick decides to walk home; on the way, he sees Owl Eyes, who has crashed his car into a ditch. Owl Eyes loudly proclaims that he is finished with the whole business; it is not clear (either to Nick or to the reader) what, if anything, he means by this.

Nick informs the reader that he did not merely attend parties during the summer of 1922; he was also working in New York, a city which he simultaneously loves and hates. At Tom and Daisy's urging, he becomes romantically involved with Jordan Baker. Though he finds her essential dishonesty somewhat off–putting, he is attracted to her despite himself.

Analysis

In this chapter, Jay Gatsby remains fundamentally a mystery. Few of the partygoers have met their host, and Gatsby stands aloof from his own celebration. He does not drink, he does not dance, he remains an observer. The man himself stands in stark contrast to the sinister gossip Nick has heard about him. Gatsby is young and handsome, with a beautiful smile that seems to radiate hope and optimism. Nick falls instantly in love with Gatsby's smile, remarking that it has "a quality of eternal reassurance in it." Gatsby's innate hopefulness is contagious.

Though Nick implies throughout the novel that wealth and ostentation tend to mask immorality and decay, Gatsby's wealth seems to serve another purpose, one that is not yet clear. The reader already knows that not everything about Gatsby is mere display: his books are real, for example, and his smile is real. However, he has a queer false English accent that is obviously false. Gatsby, at this point in the novel, remains an enigma, a creature of contradictions.

Fitzgerald gives great attention to the details of contemporary society: Gatsby's party is both a description and parody of Jazz Age decadence. It exemplifies the spirit of conspicuous consumption, and is a queer mix of the lewd and the respectable. Though catered to by butlers and serenaded by professionally trained singers, the guests are drunk, crude, and boisterous. The orchestra plays a work by Tostoff called The Jazz History of the World; though it had had a fantastic reception at Carnegie Hall, the piece is the antithesis of classical respectability.

At the time of The Great Gatsby's publication, cars were still novelty items; in the novel, they are imbued with a sense of luxurious danger. A car accident disturbs the end of the party, when a drunken man crashes his car into a ditch. Nick admonishes Jordan for being an unspeakably awful driver, and her near–accident serves as a metaphor for the behavior of her contemporaries. Jordan is a careless driver because she considers caution the responsibility of others; she feels that the onus is on them to keep out of her way.

The chapter also reinforces Nick's position an objective and reliable narrator: it ends with his claim that he is one of the few honest people he has ever known. Jordan Baker, by contrast, is compulsively dishonest; the fact that she cheated to win her first golf tournament is entirely unsurprising. She assumes that everyone else is as dishonest as she: she automatically concludes that Gatsby's books, like the better part of her own personality, exist merely for the sake of appearance.

Summary and Analysis of Chapter 4

Chapter Four

At a Sunday morning party at Gatsby's, Nick hears further gossip about Gatsby from a group of foolish young women. They say that he is a bootlegger who killed a man who discovered that he was nephew to von Hindenburg and second cousin to the devil. One morning, Gatsby invites Nick to lunch in the city. He proudly displays his Rolls–Royce, then abruptly asks Nick what he thinks of him. Nick is understandably evasive. Gatsby responds to his reticence by giving Nick an account of his past. His story, however, is highly improbable. Though he claims to descend from a prominent Midwestern family, when Nick asks him which Midwestern city he comes from, Gatsby hesitates, then says "San Francisco." He rattles off an absurdly long list of accomplishments: he claims to have studied at Oxford and lived in all of the capitals of Europe; then he enlisted in the war effort, where he was rapidly promoted to major and decorated by every Allied government, including Montenegro. He pulls out a photograph of himself in Oxford cricket whites, as well as a medal awarded by the government of Montenegro, in order to corroborate his story. They drive very fast through the valley of ashes; when Gatsby is stopped for speeding, he flashes a white card at the policeman. The policeman apologizes profusely and does not give Gatsby a ticket.

At lunch, Gatsby introduces Carraway to Meyer Wolfsheim, a disreputable character who proudly calls their attention to his cufflinks, which are made from human molars. Wolfsheim is an infamous gambler, and claims responsibility for fixing the 1919 World Series. Nick begins to suspect Gatsby of underworld dealings, due to his association with the sinister Wolfsheim.

They happen to run into Tom Buchanan, and Nick introduces him to Gatsby. Gatsby appears highly uncomfortable in Tom's presence and quickly leaves without giving an explanation.

During Nick's next encounter with Jordan Baker, she finally tells him her remarkable news: Gatsby is in love with Daisy Buchanan. Back in 1917, when Daisy was eighteen and Jordan sixteen, the two had been volunteers with the Red Cross. Though all the officers at the military base had courted Daisy, she fell passionately in love with a young lieutenant named Jay Gatsby. Though she had promised to wait for Gatsby's return, she accepted Tom Buchanan's proposal of marriage while Gatsby was still away at war. The night before her wedding, Daisy suddenly realized the enormity of her mistake; she became hysterical and drank herself into a stupor.

According to Jordan, Gatsby bought his house in West Egg just in order to be close to Daisy. It is at this moment that Nick realizes that the green light, toward which he saw Gatsby so plaintively gesturing, is the light that marks the end of the Buchanans' dock. Jordan informs Nick that Gatsby wants him to arrange a reunion between himself and Daisy.

Analysis

This chapter is primarily concerned with the mystery of Gatsby's background, and of the source of his wealth. Though Nick was first taken with Gatsby's seeming purity and optimism, Gatsby remains enigmatic and not entirely trustworthy. Gatsby's own account of his illustrious past seems comically exaggerated. His readiness to provide evidence to corroborate his story is itself suspect; an honest man, one imagines, would be insulted by Nick's skepticism.

The introduction of Meyer Wolfsheim serves to increase Nick's - and the reader's - doubts concerning Gatsby's virtue. Nick begins to suspect that the rumors of Gatsby's involvement with organized crime and bootlegging may not be entirely false.

Jordan's story about of Gatsby, by contrast, portrays him as a romantic, forced to worship his lover from afar. Although Jordan implies that there was something in Gatsby's background that caused Daisy's parents to oppose their marriage, it is clear that the young Jay Gatsby was a man of unimpeachable virtue. Fitzgerald draws upon a few centuries of romantic cliché to present Gatsby as the ideal lover: a soldier going off to war, brave and handsome, young and pure. Nick's ambivalence toward Gatsby, in which he finds himself constantly oscillating between admiration and distaste (recall that Nick found the excesses of Gatsby's party repellent), is emphasized in this chapter. The contradiction inherent in Gatsby's character between his guileless optimism and putative moral corruption is also reinforced.

It is important to note that Wolfsheim, the novel's symbolic representative of the "criminal element," is obviously Jewish: Fitzgerald gives the character a number of stereotypical physical features (a large nose, a diminutive stature) that were a staple of racist caricature in the 1920s. During this period, anti–Semitism in America was at an all–time high: Jews, as a result of their "characteristic greed," were held responsible for the corruption of the nation as a whole. Fitzgerald seems to uncritically draw on this racist ideology in his presentation of Wolfsheim; the character is nothing more than a grotesque stereotype.

This chapter also reveals the object of Gatsby's yearning which has been apparent since the first chapter: it was Daisy, and his love for Daisy, that caused him to reach out toward the mysterious green light. The green light serves as a symbol for a number of things: among them are Gatsby's dauntless romantic optimism, Daisy herself, and the American dream.

Even Gatsby's infamous parties are thrown for the sole purpose of attracting Daisy's attention; she is his animating force. Everything Gatsby does and has done is out of love for her: he has reinvented himself as a cultured millionaire solely to court her approval. In this way, Daisy seems to serve as a symbol of the American Dream (at least in its 1920s manifestation); her corruption and emptiness will reveal the corruption that has befallen the great dream itself.

Summary and Analysis of Chapter 5

Chapter Five

One night, Gatsby waylays Nick and nervously asks him if he would like to take a swim in his pool. When Nick demurs, he offers him a trip to Coney Island. Nick, initially baffled by Gatsby's solicitousness, realizes that he is anxiously waiting for Nick to arrange his meeting with Daisy. Nick agrees to do so. Gatsby, almost wild with joy, responds by offering him a job, a "confidential sort of thing," and assures Nick that he will not have to work with Meyer Wolfsheim. Nick is somewhat insulted that Gatsby wishes to reimburse him for his help, and declines Gatsby's offer.

It rains on the day that Gatsby and Daisy are to meet, and Gatsby becomes extremely apprehensive. The meeting takes place at Nick's house and, initially, their conversation is stilted and awkward. They are all inexplicably embarrassed; when Gatsby clumsily knocks over a clock, Nick tells him that he's behaving like a little boy. Nick leaves the couple alone for a few minutes. When he returns, they seem luminously happy, as though they have just concluded an embrace. There are tears of happiness on Daisy's cheeks.

They make their way over to Gatsby's mansion, of which Gatsby proceeds to give them a carefully rehearsed tour. Gatsby shows Daisy newspaper clippings detailing his exploits. She is overwhelmed by them, and by the opulence of his possessions. When he shows her his vast collection of imported shirts, she begins to weep tears of joy. Nick wonders whether Gatsby is disappointed with Daisy; it seems that he has concieved of her as a goddess, and - though Daisy is alluring, she cannot possibly live up to so grandiose an ideal.

Gatsby has Ewing Klipspringer, a mysterious man who seems to live at his mansion, play "Ain't We Got Fun" (a popular song of the time) for himself and Daisy:

> In the morning, in the evening
>
> Ain't we got fun!
>
> Got no money, but oh, honey
>
> Ain't we got fun!

As Klipspringer plays, Gatsby and Daisy draw closer and closer together. Nick, realizing that his presence has become superfluous, quietly leaves.

Analysis

The exchange between Nick and Gatsby that opens this chapter highlights the uncertainty at the heart of their relationship. Is Gatsby's friendship with Nick merely expedient? Is he merely using him to draw closer to Daisy - or is he genuinely fond of Nick?

The question cannot be easily answered: while it becomes clear that Gatsby has great affection for Nick, it is also true that he uses money and power as leverage in all of his personal relationships. Gatsby, in his extreme insecurity about class, cannot believe that anyone would befriend him if he did not possess a mansion and make several million dollars per year. Fitzgerald seems to bitterly affirm this insecurity, given the fact that Gatsby was abandoned by Daisy because of his poverty, and remains ostracized by the East Eggers even after his success. In the world of the novel, only Nick does not make friendships based upon class.

The gross materialism of the East and West Egg areas explains the obsessive care that Gatsby takes in his reunion with Daisy. The afternoon is given over to an ostentatious display of wealth: he shows Daisy his extensive collection of British antiques and takes her on a tour of his wardrobe. Gatsby himself is dressed in gold and silver. His Gothic mansion is described as looking like the citadel of a feudal lord. Nearly everything in the house is imported from England (the scene in which Gatsby shows Daisy his stock of English shirts is one of the most famous in American literature). Fitzgerald implies that Gatsby is attempting to live the life of a European aristocrat in the New World of America. This, Fitzgerald suggests, is a misguided anachronism: America committed itself to progress and equality in abandoning the old aristocracy. To go back to such rigidly defined class distinctions would be retrograde and barbaric. This is reinforced by the fact that the major proponent of such ideas is Tom Buchanan, who is clearly a brute.

This chapter presents Gatsby as a man who cannot help but live in the past: he longs to stop time, as though he and Daisy had never been separated and as though she had never left him to marry Tom. During their meeting, Nick remarks that he is acting like "a little boy." In Daisy's presence, Gatsby loses his usual debonair manner and behaves like any awkward young man in love. Gatsby himself is regressing, as though he were still a shy young soldier in love with a privileged debutante.

Nick describes the restless Gatsby as "running down like an over–wound clock." It is significant that Gatsby, in his nervousness about whether Daisy's feelings toward him have changed, knocks over Nick's clock: this signifies both Gatsby's consuming desire to stop time and his inability to do so.

Daisy, too, ceases to play the part of a world–weary sophisticate upon her reunion with Gatsby. She weeps when he shows her his collection of sumptuous English shirts, and seems genuinely overjoyed at his success. In short, Gatsby transforms her; she becomes almost human. Daisy is more sympathetic in this chapter than she is at any other point in the novel.

The song "Ain't We Got Fun" is significant for a number of reasons. The opening lyrics ("In the morning/ In the evening/ Ain't we got fun") imply a carefree spontaneity that stands in stark contrast to the tightly–controlled quality of the lovers' reunion. This contrast is further sharpened by the words of the next verse, which run: "Got no money/ But oh, honey/ Ain't we got fun!" It is bitterly ironic that Gatsby and Daisy should reunite to the strains of this song, given the fact that she rejected him because of his poverty.

Summary and Analysis of Chapter 6

Chapter Six

A reporter, inspired by the feverish gossip about Gatsby circulating in New York, comes to West Egg in hopes of obtaining the true story of his past from him. Though Gatsby himself turns the man away, Nick interrupts the narrative to relate Gatsby's past (the truth of which he only learned much later) to the reader.

His real name is James Gatz, and he was born to an impoverished farmer in North Dakota, rather than into wealth in San Francisco, as he claimed. He had his named legally changed to Jay Gatsby at the age of seventeen. Though he did attend St Olaf's, a small college in Minnesota, he dropped out after two weeks, as he could not bear working as a janitor in order to pay his tuition. Gatsby's dreams of self–improvement were only intensified by his relationship with Dan Cody, a man whom he met while working as a fisherman on Lake Superior. Cody was then fifty, a self–made millionaire who had made his fortune during the Yukon gold rush. Cody took Gatsby in and made the young man his personal assistant. On their subsequent voyages to the West Indies and the Barbary Coast, Gatsby became even more passionately covetous of wealth and privilege. When Cody died, Gatsby inherited $25,000; he was unable to claim it, however, due to the malicious intervention of Cody's mistress, Ella Kaye. Afterward, Gatsby vowed to become a success in his own right.

Several weeks pass without Nick's seeing Gatsby. Upon visiting Gatsby at his mansion, Nick is shocked to find Tom Buchanan there. Tom has unexpectedly stopped for a drink at Gatsby's after an afternoon of horseback riding; he is accompanied by Mr. and Mrs. Sloane, an insufferable East Egg couple who exemplify everything that is repellent about the "old rich." Gatsby invites the group to supper, but Mrs. Sloane hastily refuses; perhaps ashamed of her own rudeness, she then half–heartedly offers Gatsby and Nick an invitation to dine at her home. Nick, recognizing the insincerity of her offer, declines; Gatsby accepts, though it is unclear whether his gesture is truly oblivious or defiant.

Tom pointedly complains about the crazy people that Daisy meets, presumably referring to Gatsby. Throughout the awkward afternoon, he is contemptuous of Gatsby, - particularly mocking his acceptance of Mrs. Sloane's disingenuous invitation.

The following Saturday, Tom and Daisy attend one of Gatsby's parties. Tom, predictably, is unpleasant and rude throughout the evening. After the Buchanans leave, Gatsby is crestfallen at the thought that Daisy did not have a good time; he does not yet know that Tom badly upset her by telling her that Gatsby made his fortune in bootlegging.

Nick realizes that Gatsby wants Daisy to tell Tom that she has never loved him. Nick gently informs Gatsby that he cannot ask too much of Daisy, and says, "You can't repeat the past." Gatsby spiritedly replies: "Of course you can!"

Analysis

Nick begins the story of Gatsby's past by saying that Gatsby "sprang from his Platonic conception of himself," which refers to that his ideal form. That is, the Platonic form of an object is the perfect form of that object. Therefore, Nick is suggesting that Gatsby has modeled himself on an idealized version of "Jay Gatsby": he is striving to be the man he envisions in his fondest dreams of himself. Gatsby is thus the novel's representative of the American Dream, and the story of his youth borrows on one of that dream's oldest myths: that of the self–made man. In changing his name from James Gatz to Jay Gatsby, he attempts to remake himself on his own terms; Gatsby wishes to be reborn as the aristocrat he feels himself to be.

It is significant that Gatsby leaves college because he finds his work as a janitor degrading. This seems a perverse decision, given the fact that a university education would dramatically improve his social standing. His decision to leave reveals Gatsby's extreme sensitivity to class, and to the fact of his own poverty; from his childhood onward, he longs for wealth and- for the sophistication and elegance which he imagines that wealth will lend him. His work as a janitor is a gross humiliation because it is at odds with his ideal of himself; to protect that ideal, he is willing to damage his actual circumstances.

Fitzgerald uses the character of Dan Cody to subtly suggest that the America of the 1920s is no longer a place where self–made men can thrive. Cody, like Gatsby, transcended early hardship to become a millionaire. Like Gatsby, he is remarkably generous to his friends and subordinates. Cody takes to drinking because, despite his wealth, he remains unable to carve out a place for himself in the world of 1920s America. It is important to note that Cody's death is brought about, at least in part, through the treachery of the woman he loves; this foreshadows the circumstances of Gatsby's death in Chapter VIII.

The painfully awkward luncheon party at Gatsby's mansion underlines the hostility of the American 1920s toward the figure of the self–made man. Both the Sloanes and Tom Buchanan treat Gatsby with contempt and condescension, because he is not of the long–standing American upper class. Though Gatsby is fabulously wealthy, perhaps wealthier than Tom himself, he is still regarded as socially inferior. For Fitzgerald, nothing could be more inimical to the original ideals of America. The first Americans fought to escape the tyrannies of the European nobility; Tom Buchanan longs to reproduce them.

This chapter makes it clear that Daisy, too, is a part of the same narrow–minded aristocracy that produced her husband. For Gatsby, she became the symbol of everything that he wanted to possess: she is the epitome of wealth and sophistication.

Though Gatsby loves this quality in Daisy, it is precisely because she is an aristocrat that she cannot possibly fulfill his dreams. She would never sacrifice her own class status in order to be with him. Her love for him pales in comparison to her love of privilege.

Summary and Analysis of Chapter 7

Chapter Seven

At this point in the novel, when curiosity about Gatsby has reached a fever pitch, he ceases to throw his Saturday night parties. The only purpose of the parties was to solicit Daisy's attention; now that they are reunited, the parties have lost their purpose.

Nick, surprised that the revelry has stopped, goes over to make certain that Gatsby is all right. He learns that Gatsby has fired all of his former servants and replaced them with a number of disreputable characters who were formerly employed by Meyer Wolfsheim. Daisy has begun visiting him in the afternoons, and Gatsby wants to make certain that she will not be exposed to any of the lurid gossip about his life and his past.

On the hottest day of the summer, Daisy invites Gatsby, Nick, and Jordan to lunch. Daisy has the nanny exhibit her infant daughter, who is dressed in white, to the assembled guests. Gatsby seems almost bewildered by the child. He has been, until this moment, entirely unable to conceive of Daisy as a mother. Tom is full of his usual bluster, remarking that he read that the sun is growing hotter; soon, the earth will fall into it, and that will be the end of the world.

During the luncheon, Tom realizes that Gatsby and his wife are romantically involved. Gatsby stares at Daisy with undisguised passion, and Daisy recklessly remarks, within earshot of Tom, that she loves Gatsby.

Tom, unsettled, goes inside to get a drink, and in his absence Nick remarks that Daisy has an indiscreet voice. When Nick goes on to say that Daisy's voice also has an indescribably seductive quality, Gatsby blurts that her voice is "full of money."

Tom, desperate to pick a fight with Gatsby, forces the entire party to drive into New York. Gatsby and Daisy drive in Tom's car, while Nick, Jordan, and Tom drive in Gatsby's. On the way, Tom furiously tells Nick that Gatsby is no Oxford man. They stop for gas at Wilson's garage. Wilson tells them that he's decided to move his wife out west, since he recently learned that she's been having an affair; he does not yet, however, know who her lover is. Upon leaving the garage, they see Myrtle peering down at the car from her window. She stares at Jordan with an expression of jealous terror, since she assumes that Jordan is Tom's wife.

Feeling that both his wife and mistress are slipping away from him, Tom grows panicked and impatient. To escape from the summer heat, the group takes a suite at the Plaza Hotel. There, Tom finally confronts Gatsby, mocking his use of the phrase "old sport." Tom accuses Gatsby of never having been at Oxford; Gatsby replies that he did, in fact, study there for five months after the end of the war. Tom regards

Daisy's affair with the lower–class Gatsby as one of the harbingers of the decline of civilization. Soon, Tom hisses, there will even be intermarriage between the races. Gatsby tells Tom that Daisy doesn't love him, and has never loved him; he informs him that he's "not going to take care of Daisy anymore." Tom calls Gatsby a "common swindler" and reveals that he has made his fortune in bootlegging. Daisy, in her shallowness and snobbery, sides with Tom, and refuses Gatsby when he pleads with her to say that she has never loved her husband. As the confrontation draws to a close, Nick realizes that today is his thirtieth birthday.

In the valley of ashes, Nick, Jordan and Tom find that someone has been struck and killed by an automobile. The young Greek, Michaelis, who runs the coffee house next to Wilson's garage, tells them that the victim was Myrtle Wilson. She ran out into the road during a fight with her husband; there, she was struck by an opulent yellow car. Nick realizes that the fatal car must have been Gatsby's Rolls–Royce. Tom presumes that Gatsby was the driver.

Analysis

The reunion of Gatsby and Daisy is the novel's pivotal event; it sets all the subsequent events into inevitable motion. In Chapter VII, the story of their romance reaches its climax and its tragic conclusion.

Gatsby is profoundly changed by his reunion with Daisy: he ceases to throw his lavish parties and, for the first time, shows concern for his public reputation. In the past, Gatsby has simply ignored the vicious rumors circulating about him; for Daisy's sake, however, he must now exercise some discretion.

Daisy, by contrast, is extremely indiscreet with regard to her romance with Gatsby. Inviting Gatsby to lunch with her husband would be a bold, foolish move under any circumstances. When one takes Tom's snobbery and intense suspiciousness into account, Daisy's decision seems to border on madness. Tom is profoundly insecure, obsessed with both his own inevitable downfall and the downfall of civilization itself. It is important to recognize that, for Tom, they are one and the same. He believes that, as a wealthy white male aristocrat, he is Western civilization's greatest achievement. This odious mindset is borne out by his choice of reading material, which views the end of the world and interracial marriage as being equally catastrophic.

The confrontation between Gatsby and Tom serves to reveal the major flaws and motivations of both characters. For Tom, the affair between Gatsby and Daisy is evidence of the decline of civilization; he seems less disturbed by his wife's infidelity than by the fact that she is involved with a man of an inferior social class. Tom's gross misogyny and hypocrisy assert themselves with a vengeance. He obviously does not regard his affair with the even lower–class Myrtle Wilson in the same apocalyptic light. As Nick remarks, Tom moves "from libertine to prig" when it suits his needs.

Tom uses the fact of Gatsby's criminal activity to humiliate him before Daisy. Tom, for all his crudeness, possesses a subtle knowledge of his wife: he realizes that Daisy's innate snobbery is ultimately identical with his own. She would never desert her aristocratic husband for "a common bootlegger," regardless of the love she felt for the bootlegger in question. Daisy refuses to submit to Gatsby's pleas, and will not say that she has never loved Tom. Gatsby is ultimately unable to recapture his idyllic past; the past, the future, and Daisy herself ultimately belong to Tom.

The distinction between "old" and "new" money is crucial in this chapter. While Gatsby earned his fortune, Daisy is an aristocrat, a woman for whom wealth and privilege were available at birth. As Gatsby himself remarks, even her voice is "full of money." This is what he loves in Daisy's voice, and in Daisy herself: for Gatsby, Daisy represents the wealth and elegance for which he has yearned all his life. Gatsby thus loses Daisy for the same reason that he adores her: her patrician arrogance.

The introduction of Daisy's daughter provides incontestable proof of Gatsby's inability to annul the passage of time. He does not believe in the child's existence until actually confronted with her; even then, he regards her with shock and bewilderment. Daisy, for her part, seems scarcely to regard the girl as real: she coos over her as though she were a doll, and seems to leave her almost entirely in the care of a nanny. The selfish and immature Daisy is essentially a child herself, and is in no position to be a mother.

Daisy remains characteristically passive throughout Chapter VII; she is only a spectator to the argument between Gatsby and Tom. Her weakness is particularly important during this confrontation. Tom and Gatsby fight over who can possess Daisy and provide for her. Gatsby, tellingly, does not say that Daisy is leaving Tom, but that Tom is "not going to take care of her anymore"; both men regard her as being incapable of independent action.

Daisy's carelessness and stupidity eventually lead to the death of Myrtle Wilson, and Gatsby is forced to leave the scene of the accident and to hide the fatal car simply to protect Daisy's fragile nerves. His decision to take responsibility for Myrtle's death reveals that his love for Daisy is unassailable; her cruelty has changed and will change nothing. Gatsby, despite his criminal activities, remains essentially noble: he is willing to sacrifice himself for the woman he loves.

Summary and Analysis of Chapter 8

Chapter Eight

That night, Nick finds himself unable to sleep, since the terrible events of the day have greatly unsettled him. Wracked by anxiety, he hurries to Gatsby's mansion shortly before dawn. He advises Gatsby to leave Long Island until the scandal of Myrtle's death has quieted down. Gatsby refuses, as he cannot bring himself to leave Daisy: he tells Nick that he spent the entire night in front of the Buchanans' mansion, just to ensure that Daisy was safe. He tells Nick that Tom did not try to harm her, and that Daisy did not come out to meet him, though he was standing on her lawn in full moonlight.

Gatsby, in his misery, tells Nick the story of his first meeting with Daisy. He does so even though it patently gives the lie to his earlier account of his past. Gatsby and Daisy first met in Louisville in 1917; Gatsby was instantly smitten with her wealth, her beauty, and her youthful innocence. Realizing that Daisy would spurn him if she knew of his poverty, Gatsby determined to lie to her about his past and his circumstances. Before he left for the war, Daisy promised to wait for him; the two then slept together, as though to seal their pact. Of course, Daisy did not wait; she married Tom, who was her social equal and the choice of her parents.

Realizing that it has grown late, Nick says goodbye to Gatsby. As he is walking away, he turns back and shouts that Gatsby is "worth the whole damn bunch [of the Buchanans and their East Egg friends] put together."

The scene shifts from West Egg to the valley of ashes, where George Wilson has sought refuge with Michaelis. It is from the latter that Nick later learns what happened in the aftermath of Myrtle's death. George Wilson tells Michaelis that he confronted Myrtle with the evidence of her affair and told her that, although she could conceal her sin from her husband, she could not hide it from the eyes of God. As the sun rises over the valley of ashes, Wilson is suddenly transfixed by the eyes of Dr. T.J. Eckleburg; he mistakes them for the eyes of God. Wilson assumes that the driver of the fatal car was Myrtle's lover, and decides to punish this man for his sins.

He seeks out Tom Buchanan, in the hope that Tom will know the driver's identity. Tom tells him that Gatsby was the driver. Wilson drives to Gatsby's mansion; there, he finds Gatsby floating in his pool, staring contemplatively at the sky. Wilson shoots Gatsby, and then turns the gun on himself.

It is Nick who finds Gatsby's body. He reflects that Gatsby died utterly disillusioned, having lost, in rapid succession, his lover and his dreams.

Analysis

Nick gives the novel's final appraisal of Gatsby when he asserts that Gatsby is "worth the whole damn bunch of them." Despite the ambivalence he feels toward Gatsby's criminal past and nouveau riche affectations, Nick cannot help but admire him for his essential nobility. Though he disapproved of Gatsby "from beginning to end," Nick is still able to recognize him as a visionary, a man capable of grand passion and great dreams. He represents an ideal that had grown exceedingly rare in the 1920s, which Nick (along with Fitzgerald) regards as an age of cynicism, decadence, and cruelty.

Nick, in his reflections on Gatsby's life, suggests that Gatsby's great mistake was loving Daisy. He chose an inferior object upon which to focus his almost mystical capacity for dreaming. Just as the American Dream itself has degenerated into the crass pursuit of material wealth, Gatsby, too, strived only for wealth once he had fallen in love with Daisy, whose trivial, limited imagination could conceive of nothing greater. It is significant that Gatsby is not murdered for his criminal connections, but rather for his unswerving devotion to Daisy. As Nick writes, Gatsby thus "[pays] a high price for living too long with a single dream."

Up to the moment of his death, Gatsby cannot accept that his dream is over: he continues to insist that Daisy may still come to him, though it is clear to everyone, including the reader, that she is bound indissolubly to Tom. Gatsby's death thus seems almost inevitable, given that a dreamer cannot exist without his dreams; through Daisy's betrayal, he effectively loses his reason for living.

Wilson seems to be Gatsby's grim double in Chapter VIII, and represents the more menacing aspects of a capacity for visionary dreaming. Like Gatsby, he fundamentally alters the course of his life by attaching symbolic significance to something that is, in and of itself, meaningless. For Gatsby, it is Daisy and her green light, for Wilson, it is the eyes of Dr. T.J. Eckleburg. Both men are destroyed by their love of women who love the brutal Tom Buchanan; both are consumed with longing for something greater than themselves. While Gatsby is a "successful" American dreamer (at least insofar as he has realized his dreams of wealth), Wilson exemplifies the fate of the failed dreamer, whose poverty has deprived him of even his ability to hope.

Gatsby's death takes place on the first day of autumn, when a chill has begun to creep into the air. His decision to use his pool is in defiance of the change of seasons, and represents yet another instance of Gatsby's unwillingness to accept the passage of time. The summer is, for him, equivalent to his reunion with Daisy; the end of the summer heralds the end of their romance.

Summary and Analysis of Chapter 9

Chapter Nine

Like insects, reporters and gossipmongers swarm around Gatsby's mansion after his death. They immediately busy themselves with spreading grotesquely exaggerated stories about his murder, his life, and his relationships. Nick tries to give Gatsby a funeral as grand as his parties, but finds that Gatsby's enormous circle of acquaintances has suddenly evaporated. Many, like Tom and Daisy Buchanan, have simply skipped town, while others, including Meyer Wolfsheim and Kilpspringer, flatly refuse to attend the funeral.

Nick tracks down Gatsby's father, Henry C. Gatz, a solemn old man left helpless and distraught by the death of his son. Gatz shows Nick a book in which the young Gatsby kept a self–improvement schedule; nearly every minute of his day was meticulously planned. The only other attendee at Gatsby's funeral is Owl Eyes, the melancholy drunk who was so astonished by Gatsby's library.

Nick meets with Jordan Baker, who recalls their conversation about how bad drivers are only dangerous when two of them meet. She tells Nick that she and he are both "bad drivers," and are therefore a treacherous combination. When Nick ends their affair, she suddenly claims to be engaged to another man.

Months later, Nick runs into Tom Buchanan on New York's Fifth Avenue. Tom admits that it was he who sent Wilson to Gatsby's; he shows no remorse, however, and says that Gatsby deserved to die. Nick reflects that Tom and Daisy are capable only of cruelty and destruction; they are kept safe from the consequences of their actions by their fortress of wealth and privilege.

Nick, repulsed by the shallow and brutal East, determines to return to the Midwest. He reflects that he, the Buchanans, Gatsby, and Jordan are all Westerners who came east; perhaps they all possess some deficiency which makes them unsuitable to Eastern life. After Gatsby's death, the East is haunted, grotesque; the Midwest, by contrast, now seems as idyllic as a scene on a Christmas card.

Staring at the moon on his last night in West Egg, Nick imagines a primeval America, an America made for dreamers like Gatsby. The green light at the end of Daisy's dock is like the green continent of America, beckoning its legions of dreamers. Gatsby, for all his greatness, failed to realize that the American Dream was already dead when he began to dream it: his goals, the pursuit of wealth and status, had long since become empty and meaningless. Nick muses that contemporary Americans are "boats against the current, borne back ceaselessly into the past"; any attempt to progress, to move forward, is ultimately futile.

Analysis

The final line of The Great Gatsby is one of the most famous in American literature, and serves as a sort of epitaph for both Gatsby and the novel as a whole.

> So we beat on, boats against the current, borne back ceaselessly
> into the past.

Here, Nick reveals Gatsby's lifelong quest to transcend his past as ultimately futile. In comparing this backward–driving force to the current of a river, Fitzgerald presents it as both inexorable and, in some sense, naturally determined. It is the inescapable lot of humanity to move backward. Therefore, any attempt at progress is the result of hubris and outsized ambition.

Nick, in reflecting on America as a whole, links its fate to Gatsby's. America, according to Fitzgerald, was founded on the ideals of progress and equality. The America envisioned by its founders was a land made for men like Gatsby: it was intended as a place where visionary dreamers could thrive. Instead, people like Tom and Daisy Buchanan have recreated the excesses of the European aristocracy in the New World. Gatsby, for all his wealth and greatness, could not become a part of their world; his noble attempt to engineer his own destiny was sabotaged by their cruelty and by the stunted quality of their imaginations. Fitzgerald's America is emphatically not a place where anything is possible: just as America has failed to transcend its European origins, Gatsby, too, cannot overcome the circumstances of his upbringing.

Though Nick worships Gatsby's courage and capacity for self–reinvention, he cannot approve of either his dishonesty or his criminal dealings. Gatsby, both while he is alive and after his death, poses an insoluble challenge to Nick's customary ways of thinking about the world. Nick firmly believes that the past determines who we are: he suggests that he, and all the novel's characters, are fundamentally Westerners, and thus intrinsically unsuited to life in the East. The West, though it was once emblematic of the American desire for progress, is presented in the novel's final pages as the seat of traditional morality, an idyllic heartland, in stark contrast to the greed and depravity of the East.

It is important to note that the Buchanans lived in East Egg, and Gatsby in West Egg; therefore, in gazing at the green light on Daisy's dock, Gatsby was looking East. The green light, like the green land of America itself, was once a symbol of hope; now, the original ideals of the American dream have deteriorated into the crass pursuit of wealth. In committing his extraordinary capacity for dreaming to his love for Daisy, Gatsby, too, devoted himself to nothing more than material gain. In Fitzgerald's grim version of the Roaring Twenties, Gatsby's ruin both mirrors and prefigures the ruin of America itself.

Suggested Essay Questions

1. Analyze Fitzgerald's conception of the American Dream. Does he view it as totally dead, or is it possible to revive it?
2. Is Nick a reliable narrator? How does his point of view color the reality of the novel, and what facts or occurences would he have a vested interest in obscuring?
3. Trace the use of the color white in the novel. When does it falsify a sense of innocence? When does it symbolize true innocence?
4. Do a close reading of the description of the "valley of ashes." How does Fitzgerald use religious imagery in this section of the novel?
5. What does the green light symbolize to Gatsby? To Nick?
6. How does Fitzgerald juxtapose the different regions of America? Does he write more positively about the East or the Midwest?
7. What is the distinction between East and West Egg? How does one bridge the gap between the two?
8. In what ways are Wilson and Gatsby similar? Disimilar? Who is Nick more sympathetic to?
9. How does Fitzgerald treat New York City? What is permissable in the urban space that is taboo on the Eggs?
10. Is Tom most responsible for Gatsby's death? Daisy? Myrtle? Gatsby himself? Give reasons why or why not each character is implicated in the murder.

Suggested Essay Questions

Fitzgerald and the Lost Generation

Although The Great Gatsby is generally considered to be a work focused on the American Dream and is analyzed as such, it has connections to other literary work of its period. The Great Gatsby's publication in 1925 put it at the forefront of literary work by a group which began to be called the Lost Generation. The group was so–called because of the existential questioning that began to occur in American literature for the first time after the war. Many critics argue that this Generation marked the first mature body of literature to come from the United States.

The Lost Generation more specifically was a group of writers and artists who lived and worked in Paris or in other parts of Europe during World War I and the Depression. This group included authors such as F. Scott Fitzgerald, Ernest Hemingway, Ezra Pound, and T.S. Eliot. This group often had social connections with one another, and would even meet to critique one another's work.

Aside from the loss of innocence caused by the first World War, the group, for the most part, shared the stylistic bond of literary modernism. Influenced by turn–of–the–century decadent poets and aestheticism (which proclaims the doctrine of "art for art's sake"), the modernist movement was a move away from realism. Instead, characters' subjective experiences were portrayed through stream–of–consciousness techniques, symbolism, or disjointed time frames. The Great Gatsby is an early exemplar of the modernist techniques of the Lost Generation, illustrating a type of jumbled symbolism in the first image of Gatsby and in the description of the "valley of ashes."

Fitzgerald and the Lost Generation

Author of ClassicNote and Sources

Jeremy Ross, author of ClassicNote. Completed on February 04, 2000, copyright held by GradeSaver.

Updated and revised Rachel Nolan September 08, 2006. Copyright held by GradeSaver.

Bernard Tanner. Fitzgerald's Odyssey: a reader's guide to the Gospels in The Great Gatsby. Lanham, MD: University Press of America, 2003.

Dalton Gross. Understanding The Great Gatsby. Westport, CT: Greenwood Press, 1998.

Matthew Bruccoli. Getting It Wrong: Resetting The Great Gatsby. Columbia, SC: s.n., 2005.

Essay: Foreshadowing Destiny

by Olivia Verma
October 18, 1995

> "Gaudy primary colors and hair shorn in strange new ways and
> shawls beyond the wildest dreams of Castille. . . The air is alive
> with chatter and laughter, and casual innuendo and introductions
> forgotten on the spot, and the enthusiastic meetings between
> women who never knew each other's names. . . The party has
> begun."

The beauty and splendor of Gatsby's parties masks the decay and corruption that lay
at the heart of the Roaring Twenties. The society of the Jazz Age, as observed by
Fitzgerald, is morally bankrupt, and thus continually plagued by a crisis of character.
Jay Gatsby, though he struggles to be a part of this world, remains unalterably an
outsider. His life is a grand irony, in that it is a caricature of Twenties–style
ostentation: his closet overflows with custom–made shirts; his lawn teems with "the
right people," all engaged in the serious work of absolute triviality; his mannerisms
(his false British accent, his old–boy friendliness) are laughably affected. Despite all
this, he can never be truly a part of the corruption that surrounds him: he remains
intrinsically "great." Nick Carrway reflects that Gatsby's determination, his lofty
goals, and - most importantly - the grand character of his dreams sets him above his
vulgar contemporaries. F. Scott Fitzgerald constructs Gatsby as a true American
dreamer, set against the decay of American society during the 1920s. This is the
same world that produced what Gertrude Stein called the "Lost Generation"; this is
the same world that T.S. Eliot condemned in "The Wasteland." By eulogizing the
tragic fate of dreamers, Fitzgerald thereby denounces 1920s America as an age of
blindness and greed - an age hostile to the work of dreaming. In *The Great Gatsby*,
Fitzgerald heralds the ruin of his own generation.

Since America has always held its entrepreneurs in the highest regard, one might
expect Fitzgerald to glorify this heroic version of the American Dreamer in the pages
of his novel. Instead, Fitzgerald suggests that the societal corruption which prevailed
in the 1920s was uniquely inhospitable to dreamers; in fact, it was these men who led
the most unfortunate lives of all. The figure of Dan Cody exemplifies the hardships
faced by the dreamer. Cody is a miner, "a product of the Nevada silver fields, of the
Yukon, of every rush for metal since seventy–five." He becomes a millionaire
through hard work, ambition and a little bit of fine American luck. Despite these
admirable qualities, he dies alone, drunk, and betrayed. Through Dan Cody,
Fitzgerald suggests that 1920s society manipulates its visionaries, milks them for
their hard–earned money, and then, promptly forgets them.

This formula is reiterated through the story of Gatsby. A child growing up in a
nameless town in the middle of Minnesota, Gatsby dreams of the impossible - and

makes the impossible a reality. He begins this grand undertaking in an endearingly methodical way: he makes a list of "General Resolves: Study electricity, baseball, practice elocution and how to attain it. . . " Less than two decades later, he is one of the richest men in New York. Gatsby, too, is exploited by the very society of which he longs to become a part. At his own parties, "Girls were swooning backward playfully into men's arms, even into groups, knowing that someone would arrest their falls – – – but no one swooned backward on Gatsby, and no French bob touched Gatsby's shoulder, and no singing quartets were formed with Gatsby's head for a link." His home was full of the Leeches, Blackbucks, Ferets and Klipspringers - or at least it was while the champagne was flowing, at Gatsby's expense. When he dies, no one attends his funeral: Gatsby dies alone, and only a handful of people mourn his passing. In a healthy society, dreamers are respected and encouraged; in Fitzgerald's version of the American Twenties, they are exploited, maltreated, and discarded. For Fitzgerald, the destruction of dreams is the hallmark of his lost generation.

Another symptom of the decline of American society is its inability to fulfill its dreamers' desires. As a child, Gatsby dreams of wealth and success - in this way, he hopes to become a part of the social elite. When Gatsby finally invites members of that elite (as exemplified by the Sloans and Buchanans) to his home, they have nothing but contempt for him. After Gatsby accepts Mrs. Sloan's invitation to dinner, the entire party rebukes him behind his back. They leave without him, hissing that they "couldn't possibly wait." Though Gatsby is now wealthy and successful, the hypocritical division between those with "new money" and those with "old money" keeps him, despite all his striving, barred from high society.

Gatsby's longing for Daisy - which is, of course, inseparable from his desire to be a part of her social class - is another dream that remains unfulfilled. Since Daisy initially refused to marry him because of his poverty and low birth, Gatsby resolved to elevate himself. It never occurs to him to condemn her for her cruelty, nor for her indefensible snobbery; instead, Gatsby strives to live up to her misconceived ideal. His idea of Daisy is of a woman pure, a woman perfect - as clear as a green light in June. When he and Daisy are reunited after a five year separation, Nick incisively remarks, "There must have been times that afternoon when Daisy tumbled short of his dreams. No amount of fire or freshness can challenge what a man will store up in his ghostly heart." Daisy is tainted by her association with the brutal and loutish Tom; she is, in fact, more like him than she is like the idealistic Gatsby. During this first meeting, Fitzgerald focuses on the fact that she is no longer dressed completely in white: "her brass buttons glint in the sunlight." She is not "the grail" that Gatsby has sought - nor will he ever find it. Daisies are seasonal flowers - they decay in the heat (the passion) of summer. Fitzgerald uses Daisy as an emblem of "old money's" pompous hypocrisy: it can never be equal to Gatsby's dreams.

The tragedy of Gatsby's life - a tragedy that is painfully clear to Nick - remains invisble to the rest of society. Blindness is one of the novel's central theme: it is populated almost entirely with people who wish not to see. They seek out blindness in the form of drunkenness: Daisy binges on alcohol the night before her wedding, in order to obliterate her vision of a miserable future. Jordan, Daisy, Tom and the other "jet–setters" of the 1920s drive recklessly; they remain blind to danger, so caught up are they with the selfish pursuit of pleasure. They thoughtlessly risk their own lives and the lives of others. Nick says to Jordan, "You're a rotten driver. Either you ought to be more careful, or you oughtn't drive." Jordan responds, "They'll keep out of my way. It takes two to make an accident." For Fitzgerald, Twenties society was "driving on toward death through the cooling twilight." Only Nick - who is, above all else, an *observer* (the novel is, in some sense, his memoir, and thus a collection of his observations) - truly *sees*. He is Fitzgerald's representative within the narrative.

Throughout the novel, Fitzgerald heralds the decay of his generation. During the climactic confrontation between Tom and Gatsby, when Gatsby learns that Daisy will never be his, Nick muses, "I just remembered it's my thirtieth birthday." This signifies the end of the corrupt lifestyle of the Twenties; now is the dawn of the Thirties. The characters attempt to escape the calamity represented by the end of the decade by moving West, away from the decaying East. Tom and Daisy leave New York, in an attempt to escape the violence they themselves have caused; Nick remarks, "They smashed up things and creatures and then retreated away. . . " America was once a land meant for dreamers; now, the mindless pursuit of wealth has destroyed the American dream. Fitzgerald saw a society hurtling recklessly onward, without direction, unwilling to take responsibility for its actions; for him, this represented the annihilation of the very fabric of America. His book was meant as a grim harbinger of that destruction.

Essay: The Eulogy of a Dream

by James Boo
April 20, 2002

The central theme of *The Great Gatsby* is the decay of the American Dream.
Through his incisive analysis - and condemnation - of 1920s high society, Fitzgerald
(in the person of the novel¹s narrator, Nick Carraway) argues that the American
Dream no longer signifies the noble pursuit of progress; instead, it has become
grossly materialistic and corrupt. Fitzgerald¹s novel is structured as an allegory (a
story that conceals another story): the terrible death of Jay Gatsby is, by extension,
the death of the American Dream.

For Fitzgerald, the true American Dream is characterized by a spirit of perseverance
and hope; through these, one can succeed against all odds. This ideal is embodied by
the young Gatsby (then James Gatz): he meticulously plans the path by which he will
become a great man in his "Hopalong Cassidy" journal - and then follows it, to the
letter. When Mr Gatz shows the tattered book to Nick, he declares, "'Jimmy was
bound to get ahead. He always had some resolves like this or something. Do you
notice what he's got about improving his mind? He was always great for that'." The
journal exemplifies the continual struggle for self−improvement that once
represented the American ideal. In comparing the young James Gatz to the young
Benjamin Franklin, Fitzgerald suggests that the American Dream does survive
despite the decay of modern society - there will always be those guided by an
indomitable hope. Modern society, however, has no place for such dreamers:
Gatsby¹s passionate desire to win Daisy's love ultimately remains unrealized, and in
fact leads to his destruction. Gatsby is first seen late at night, "standing with his
hands in his pockets"; Nick says, only half in jest, that he is "out to determine what
share [is] his of our local heavens." Nick watches Gatsby's movements and
comments:

> "He stretched out his arms toward the dark water in a curious way,
> and as far as I was from him I could swear he was trembling.
> Involuntarily I glanced seaward −− and distinguished nothing
> except a single green light, minute and far away, that might have
> been the end of the dock."

Gatsby's dedication to an ethereal ideal elevates him above his shallow, vulgar
contemporaries. His longing for Daisy is like that celebrated by the medieval ideal of
courtly love, in which a knight worshipped his lady without any hope of being loved
in return; his every action was only for her, and he strove to lead a noble life in the
hopes of becoming worthy of her. Daisy is Gatsby¹s ideal: we first see him reaching
toward the green light that marks her house in East Egg; in the final days of his life,
he waits unwearyingly outside Daisy's house for hours - despite the fact that she has
already decided to abandon him. Though Gatsby exemplifies the purest elements of

the old dream, he cannot help but fail in his pursuit of it, since the woman he loves is a corrupt product of modern society.

For Fitzgerald, the American obsession with wealth, power, and privilege is the chief cause of the decay of dreaming. Gatsby earns his money through illegal practices; his ostentatious parties, garish mansion, and lavish clothing are all attempts to win the attention of the cruel and shallow Daisy, who cares only for money. He ceases to throw his parties once he believes that he and Daisy will be reunited. Daisy and Tom Buchanan are the most detestable exemplars of the modern order: they live without hope and without regret, because all they care for is the preservation of their own power and privilege. Daisy is never heard from again after Gatsby's death, as she wants only to forget him and their relationship. Nick confronts Tom about his responsibility for Gatsby's death. Tom lies to George Wilson, telling him that Gatsby was driving the car that struck Myrtle, though Daisy was the driver; he lets George believe that Gatsby was having an affair with Myrtle, when in fact it was Tom himself. Tom scoffs at Nick: "'I told him [George] the truth... What if I did tell him? That fellow [Gatsby] had it coming to him'." Tom admits that he is responsible for Gatsby's murder and Wilson's suicide, but does not feel guilty; he has never known guilt or shame, since his position as a member of the established elite protects him from punishment. Through Nick, Fitzgerald condemns all of "high society":

> "I couldn't forgive him or like him but I saw what he had done
> was, to him, entirely justified... They were careless people, Tom
> and Daisy– they smashed up things and creatures and then
> retreated back into their money or their vast carelessness or
> whatever it was that kept them together, and let other people clean
> up the mess they had made... "

Nick realizes that Tom and Daisy represent a class that has attained success at the cost of their own dehumanization. They are a kind of social void - a wholly negative force that is capable of spreading only destruction.

Toward the end of the novel, Fitzgerald creates a sense of utter hopelessness and despair through the introduction of Tom and Daisy's child, the murder of Gatsby, and Wilson's suicide. The first hint of the impending tragedy can be found in the person of the Buchanans' daughter, whom Daisy nauseatingly refers to as "Bles–sed pre–cious." When the girl is brought into the Buchanans' salon, Nick observes Gatsby's obvious discomfort: "Gatsby and I in turn leaned down and took the small reluctant hand. Afterwards he kept looking at the child with surprise. I don't think he had ever really believed in its existence before." Daisy then calls her child an "absolute little dream," crushing all hopes Gatsby has of truly returning to the past he shares with her. The gross materialism that has taken the place of the American Dream is revealed shortly thereafter, when Nick and Gatsby attempt to discern why Daisy's voice is so seductive. Gatsby blurts out, "'Her voice is full of money'"; Nick has a sudden epiphany, which alters his view of society as a whole:

"That was it. I'd never understood before. It was full of money—
that was the inexhaustible charm that rose and fell in it, the jingle
of it, the cymbals' song of it... High in a white palace the king's
daughter, the golden girl..."

At this point, all of Daisy is stripped of all her charm and beauty; nothing remains but the coarse lure of wealth. The ideal that Gatsby has been so inexhaustibly pursuing is not love - it is money, soulless money, that has been given a deceptively pretty human face. When Gatsby dies, any chance the American Dream has of surviving in the dehumanized modern world dies with him. Nick later conjectures that Gatsby, at the moment of his death, "must have looked up at an unfamiliar sky through frightening leaves and shivered as he found what a grotesque thing a rose is and how raw the sunlight was upon the scarcely created grass." The hopes and dreams which have strengthened Gatsby and guided him are shattered as he lies bleeding in the pool; he must take leave of a world which no longer has a place for men like him. George Wilson - who symbolizes the common man struggling to eke out his own meager success on the modern world's harsh terms - commits suicide. The deaths of Gatsby and Wilson, both striving toward different versions of the original American dream, mirror the death of that dream itself. At the end of the novel, Nick returns to the Midwest with this disturbing knowledge: the American people must struggle to keep from losing its humanity: "So we beat on, boats against the current, borne back ceaselessly into the past." The dream is now utterly lost and can never be resurrected - at least not in its original, its purest form.

Through the story of a doomed romance, Fitzgerald heralds the tragic decline of American values. Gatsby and the other characters of the novel act as mere vessels for the author's true story: the American Dream, once a pure and mighty ideal, has been degraded and buried by the dehumanizing lust for money. Nick Carraway is an outsider to his own story: he is an honest man, an observer who bears witness to the calamity. *The Great Gatsby* is not, in the final analysis, a eulogy for a man named Jay Gatsby; instead, it serves as a eulogy for the idea of America itself.

Quiz 1

1. **When was The Great Gatsby published?**
   A. 1921
   B. 1922
   C. 1923
   D. 1925

2. **Who is Meyer Wolfsheim?**
   A. A wealthy man who gained his fortune from the gold rush
   B. Greek man and neighbor of Wilson who consoles him after Myrtle is killed
   C. A poor man content in his existence until he suspects that his wife is having an affair
   D. A notorious underworld figure involved in organized crime

3. **Who is Ewing Klipspringer?**
   A. A boarder who lives in Gatsby's house
   B. A guest at Gatsby's parties who wrecks his car there
   C. A longtime friend of Daisy
   D. The brother of Myrtle Wilson who lives in New York City

4. **Where did Nick Carraway attend school?**
   A. Harvard
   B. Columbia
   C. Princeton
   D. Yale

5. **Who narrarates the Great Gatsby?**
   A. Nick Carraway
   B. George Wilson
   C. Jay Gatsby
   D. Tom Buchanan

6. **Which of this things is NOT symbolized by the green light?**
   A. nature
   B. optimism
   C. The American Dream
   D. money

7. Who is Dr. Eckleburg?

A. A guest at Gatsby's party

B. Gatsby's doctor and professional associate

C. An eye doctor whose billboard overlooks the road to West Egg

D. Tom Buchanan's spy and confidante

8. The road between West Egg and East Egg is

A. A "valley of ashes"

B. A literary allusion to the mythological River Styx

C. A literary allusion to the Waste Land, by T.S. Eliot

D. All of these

9. Myrtle Wilson is

A. Daisy's friend and a golf pro

B. Nick's girlfriend

C. Tom's lover

D. The plumber's wife

10. Why do Nick and Tom go to the "valley of ashes"?

A. Tom wants Nick to meet his mistress

B. Tom's car has a transmission problem

C. Tom and Nick are passing through, on the way to Gatsby's garden party

D. None of these

11. Who claims to be in the "artistic game"?

A. Myrtle

B. Mr. McKee

C. Mrs. McKee

D. Tom

12. Why does Tom break Myrtle's nose?

A. He finds out she's having an affair with another man

B. She says Daisy's name

C. Tom tries to punch Nick and misses

D. None of these

13. What reason does Myrtle give for having an affair?

    A. "You can't live forever."

    B. "My husband, Tom, beats me. He broke my nose."

    C. "The Jazz Age is a time of irresponsibility and gaiety."

    D. "Do what you can to be happy."

14. Jay Gatsby is a

    A. Murderer

    B. German spy

    C. Bootlegger

    D. Long–time member of East Egg's elite

15. Which of these details is true about Gatsby's past?

    A. He received a degree from Oxford

    B. He's the son of wealthy people from the Midwest

    C. He fought in the war

    D. All of these are false

16. Complete the analogy. Gatsby loves Daisy like...

    A. Tom loves Daisy

    B. Tom loves Myrtle

    C. Nick loves Jordan

    D. None of these

17. Meyer Wolfsheim's cufflinks are made from

    A. egyptian gold

    B. elephant tusk

    C. obsidian

    D. human molars

18. Why does Gatsby throw extravagant parties?

    A. It diverts some attention away from his notorious crime–laden life.

    B. He hopes to make many friends.

    C. He wants to live a lavish life.

    D. He believes that Daisy may come to a party some night.

19. **Why does Nick think that Gatsby may be disappointed with Daisy?**

    A. She married Tom instead of marrying Gatbsy because Tom had more money.

    B. Daisy could not possibly live up to the dreams that Gatsby had about her.

    C. She is unimpressed by the picture of Dan Cody and Gatsby on the yacht.

    D. She does not really love Gatsby anymore.

20. **How does Gatsby dress for his first meeting with Daisy?**

    A. Black slacks, white shirt and white jacket

    B. In a striped suit

    C. In gold and silver

    D. In a pure white tuxedo with a daisy in the lapel

21. **When Gatsby and Daisy meet in Nick's home, Gatsby almost breaks Nick's**

    A. window

    B. bust of Apollo

    C. porcelain statuette

    D. clock

22. **Which of these is a reminder of the issues of money and class in the novel?**

    A. Nick's favorite color

    B. Tom's need for an affair

    C. The song that Klipspringer plays on the piano

    D. Daisy's little girl

23. **When did James Gatz change his name to Gatsby?**

    A. age 24

    B. age 17

    C. age 27

    D. age 15

24. **How is the true story of Gatsby's life revealed?**

    A. A reporter comes to Gatsby's home and interviews him. Thereafter, the rumors about Gatsby's past are compared by the narrator to the true events of Gatsby's life.

    B. Gatsby breaks down when he sees Daisy. She asks him point–blank to explain his situation to Tom and he does.

    C. Nick finds papers in Gatsby's study, then asks Gatsby to explain. At first, Gatsby is angry about the accusation of being a liar, but then confides all.

    D. Daisy pressures him into confiding it to Nick. She needs advice about Gatsby and wants Nick to know the whole story.

25. **Who changed Gatsby's life forever, inspiring him to become rich and powerful?**
     A. Dan Cody
     B. Meyer Wolfsheim
     C. Nick
     D. Daisy

Quiz 1 Answer Key

1. **(D)** 1925
2. **(D)** A notorious underworld figure involved in organized crime
3. **(A)** A boarder who lives in Gatsby's house
4. **(D)** Yale
5. **(A)** Nick Carraway
6. **(A)** nature
7. **(C)** An eye doctor whose billboard overlooks the road to West Egg
8. **(D)** All of these
9. **(C)** Tom's lover
10. **(A)** Tom wants Nick to meet his mistress
11. **(B)** Mr. McKee
12. **(B)** She says Daisy's name
13. **(A)** "You can't live forever."
14. **(C)** Bootlegger
15. **(C)** He fought in the war
16. **(D)** None of these
17. **(D)** human molars
18. **(D)** He believes that Daisy may come to a party some night.
19. **(B)** Daisy could not possibly live up to the dreams that Gatsby had about her.
20. **(C)** In gold and silver
21. **(D)** clock
22. **(C)** The song that Klipspringer plays on the piano
23. **(B)** age 17
24. **(A)** A reporter comes to Gatsby's home and interviews him. Thereafter, the rumors about Gatsby's past are compared by the narrator to the true events of Gatsby's life.
25. **(A)** Dan Cody

Quiz 2

1. **What does Gatsby want from his relationship with Daisy?**
   A. One meeting was enough for Gatsby; his dream has been fulfilled.
   B. He is satisfied only if Daisy renounces any feelings for Tom and says that she has never loved Tom.
   C. He is satisfied if Daisy leaves her husband.
   D. He is satisfied if Daisy and himself remain lovers, although he is fine with Daisy remaining married to Tom.

2. **Why is Tom angry at lunch?**
   A. He finds out that Daisy is having an affair with Gatsby, someone Tom thinks is wealthier and classier than he is.
   B. He finds out that Daisy knows about his affair with Myrtle.
   C. He finds out that Daisy is having an affair with Gatsby, someone Tom thinks is low–class.
   D. He finds out that Nick re–introduced Gatsby and Daisy.

3. **What is the significance of Nick realizing that "today is his thirtieth birthday?"**
   A. Makes an allusion between the end of the blissful twenties and the end of the blissful ignorance of the truth by Gatsby, Daisy and Tom.
   B. Shows that Nick feels disappointed that no one remebered his birthday because of all the commotion.
   C. Shows that Nick is not interested in the conflicts between the lovers and the married people; he is just thinking about his own affairs.
   D. All of these

4. **Why does Gatsby stop throwing parties?**
   A. He's tired of being leeched on by strangers; he'd rather spend the money on Daisy.
   B. He's running out of money, and he needs to retain some now that he and Daisy want to get married.
   C. He's been reunited with Daisy so he no longer needs to.
   D. He doesn't want the gossip about him to increase.

5. **Who kills Myrtle?**
   A. Gatsby
   B. George Wilson
   C. Tom
   D. Daisy

6. **Who kills Gatsby?**
   A. George Wilson
   B. Tom

C. Nick

D. Daisy

7. **Which of these lines best explains the error in Gatsby's thinking?**
     A. "In the morning, in the evening, ain't we got fun?"
     B. His voice is "full of money."
     C. His constant use of the words "old sport."
     D. "Of course you can [repeat the past]!"

8. **Why is Daisy's daughter a symbol?**
     A. She is a symbol of time passing and things changing.
     B. She is innocent and manipulated, like Gatsby.
     C. She is a symbol of Gatsby's immaturity.
     D. She is a plaything of the "nouveau riche"

9. **Why does Gatsby allow Daisy to drive his car?**
     A. She wants to murder Myrtle Wilson, her husband's mistress.
     B. Gatsby sees a symbolic sexuality in allowing Daisy to drive.
     C. She wants to calm her nerves after a tense lunch.
     D. None of these.

10. **Why doesn't Gatsby leave West Egg after Nick tells him that the authorities know that his car killed Myrtle?**
     A. He wants to protect Daisy and see what she will do.
     B. He wants to go to jail; perhaps Daisy will love him more if he gives up everything for her.
     C. He recognizes the class differences between the Wilsons and himself and thinks they would be powerless in a court of law.
     D. He thinks he has enough power to pay off the police if he faces any criminal action.

11. **Why does Nick say, "You're worth the whole damn bunch put together"?**
     A. He recognizes Gatsby's immense wealth and points out that he is worth more money than all the others combined.
     B. He admires Gatsby's vast bravery, honor, and above all optimism and faith in the American Dream.
     C. He's being sarcastic; really he thinks Gatsby is a low−life crook who deserves time behind bars.
     D. He's trying to make Gatsby feel better since he is about to go to jail.

12. **Who symbolizes God in this story?**
     A. Gatsby
     B. Wilson
     C. Nick
     D. A billboard

13. **Who does not attend Gatsby's funeral?**
    A. Owl–Eyes
    B. Meyer Wolfsheim
    C. Nick
    D. All of these men attended Gatsby's funeral.

14. **What reason does Fitzgerald give for Gatsby's death?**
    A. He "stole from the rich and gave to the poor."
    B. He never "helped build up the country."
    C. He "paid a high price for living too long with a single dream."
    D. He's "worth the whole damn bunch of them."

15. **What symbol at the end of the novel contradicts Gatsby's fervent belief that one can escape his origins and rewrite his past?**
    A. "So we beat on, boats against the current, borne ceaselessly into the past."
    B. Gatsby's death shows that you die when you try to escape the fate of your origins.
    C. Daisy wilts.
    D. The green light across the bay burns out.

16. **Where do the noveau riche live?**
    A. East Egg
    B. West Egg
    C. Central Egg
    D. New York City

17. **Tom's apartment is in**
    A. Morningside Heights
    B. East Egg
    C. the Bronx
    D. the Upper East Side

18. **Gatsby's mansion is**
    A. Gothic
    B. purple
    C. Romanesque
    D. Tudor

19. **Nick is Daisy's**
    A. cousin
    B. husband
    C. brother
    D. lover

20. **What gift does Tom give Myrtle?**
    A. a wedding band
    B. a house
    C. jewelry
    D. a dog

21. **Who does Wilson think is his wife's lover?**
    A. Jordan
    B. Gatsby
    C. Tom
    D. Nick

22. **Where does Nick meet Gatsby?**
    A. in the Midwest
    B. during the war
    C. at his own party
    D. at Oxford

23. **Where does Gatsby claim to be from?**
    A. San Francisco
    B. England
    C. Montenegro
    D. Egypt

24. **What sort of accent does Gatsby affect?**
    A. English
    B. Western
    C. Scottish
    D. Irish

25. **Why is Owl Eyes surprised by Gatsby's library?**
    A. the books are real
    B. it is on fire
    C. there is a trapdoor
    D. it contains German metals

Quiz 2 Answer Key

1. **(B)** He is satisfied only if Daisy renounces any feelings for Tom and says that she has never loved Tom.
2. **(C)** He finds out that Daisy is having an affair with Gatsby, someone Tom thinks is low–class.
3. **(A)** Makes an allusion between the end of the blissful twenties and the end of the blissful ignorance of the truth by Gatsby, Daisy and Tom.
4. **(C)** He's been reunited with Daisy so he no longer needs to.
5. **(D)** Daisy
6. **(A)** George Wilson
7. **(D)** "Of course you can [repeat the past]!"
8. **(A)** She is a symbol of time passing and things changing.
9. **(C)** She wants to calm her nerves after a tense lunch.
10. **(A)** He wants to protect Daisy and see what she will do.
11. **(B)** He admires Gatsby's vast bravery, honor, and above all optimism and faith in the American Dream.
12. **(D)** A billboard
13. **(B)** Meyer Wolfsheim
14. **(C)** He "paid a high price for living too long with a single dream."
15. **(A)** "So we beat on, boats against the current, borne ceaselessly into the past."
16. **(A)** East Egg
17. **(A)** Morningside Heights
18. **(A)** Gothic
19. **(A)** cousin
20. **(D)** a dog
21. **(B)** Gatsby
22. **(C)** at his own party
23. **(A)** San Francisco
24. **(A)** English
25. **(A)** the books are real

Quiz 3

1. **What promise did Daisy break?**
    A. that she would learn to drive
    B. that she would wait for Gatsby
    C. that she would marry Tom
    D. that she would marry Nick

2. **Where are Gatsby's shirts from?**
    A. England
    B. New York
    C. the Midwest
    D. Paris

3. **Why did Gatsby drop out of college?**
    A. he met Tom
    B. he refused to work as a janitor to support the fees
    C. the war broke out
    D. he met Daisy

4. **Which woman wears the darkest colors in the novel?**
    A. Jordan
    B. Myrtle
    C. Daisy
    D. Daisy's child

5. **The novel is set during**
    A. the Vietnam War
    B. WWI
    C. WWII
    D. Prohibition

6. **What does Gatsby say Daisy's voice sounds like?**
    A. the ocean
    B. a telephone
    C. music
    D. money

7. **Who did Daisy lose her virginity to?**
   A. Gatsby
   B. Wilson
   C. Tom
   D. Nick

8. **What is Wilson's profession?**
   A. farmer
   B. mechanic
   C. bootlegger
   D. hedge fund manager

9. **How does Gatsby die?**
   A. cancer
   B. he is murdered
   C. suicide
   D. accident

10. **What proof does Gatsby have of his fictional past?**
    A. a medal from the government of Montenegro
    B. a false passport
    C. a false moustache
    D. a Yale degree

11. **Meyer Wolfsheim is rumored to**
    A. killed Gatsby
    B. have fixed the 1919 World Series
    C. begun a genocide
    D. ended Prohibition

12. **Many of the rumors surrounding Gatsby connect him with which country?**
    A. England
    B. Germany
    C. Austria
    D. Japan

13. **At the end of the novel, Nick decides to move to**
     A. London
     B. East Egg
     C. the Midwest
     D. New York City

14. **What color car does Gatsby drive?**
     A. purple
     B. yellow
     C. green
     D. white

15. **What sport does Jordan play professionally?**
     A. soccer
     B. tennis
     C. squash
     D. golf

16. **Who were classmates?**
     A. Tom and Gatsby
     B. Nick and Gatsby
     C. Nick and Tom
     D. Tom and Daisy

17. **What does Myrtle do for a living?**
     A. interior decorator
     B. cleaning lady
     C. housewife
     D. prostitute

18. **Gatsby is first presented as a**
     A. romantic
     B. murderer
     C. religious figure
     D. fraud

19. Gatsby is later represented as a

A. romantic
B. murderer
C. adulterer
D. cynic

20. Nick is

A. married
B. divorced
C. unmarried
D. homosexual

21. When Gatsby is murdered, he is

A. in a car
B. in a pool
C. in the city
D. at Tom's house

22. What does Gatsby provide for free at his parties?

A. prostitutes
B. alcohol
C. photos of Daisy
D. books

23. Who is the most cynical person in the novel?

A. Jordan
B. Gatsby
C. Tom
D. Daisy

24. Who is the most overtly racist person in the novel?

A. Jordan
B. Gatsby
C. Tom
D. Nick

25. What does Tom see as cause for an apocalypse?
    A. republicanism
    B. interracial marriage
    C. same–sex marriage
    D. interracial friendship

Quiz 3 Answer Key

1. **(B)** that she would wait for Gatsby
2. **(A)** England
3. **(B)** he refused to work as a janitor to support the fees
4. **(B)** Myrtle
5. **(D)** Prohibition
6. **(D)** money
7. **(A)** Gatsby
8. **(B)** mechanic
9. **(B)** he is murdered
10. **(A)** a medal from the government of Montenegro
11. **(B)** have fixed the 1919 World Series
12. **(B)** Germany
13. **(C)** the Midwest
14. **(B)** yellow
15. **(D)** golf
16. **(C)** Nick and Tom
17. **(C)** housewife
18. **(C)** religious figure
19. **(A)** romantic
20. **(C)** unmarried
21. **(B)** in a pool
22. **(B)** alcohol
23. **(A)** Jordan
24. **(C)** Tom
25. **(B)** interracial marriage

Quiz 4

1. **What does Jordan claim when Nick breaks up with her?**
    A. that she is engaged to someone else
    B. that she is pregnant with his child
    C. that she is pregnant with Tom's child
    D. that she always hated him

2. **What does Tom accuse Gatsby of?**
    A. illegal activities
    B. marrying Daisy
    C. having an illegitimate child
    D. marrying Jordan

3. **Why does Wilson want to move?**
    A. he has found out that his wife is having an affair
    B. he hates Gatsby
    C. he hates Tom
    D. he wants to see China

4. **Myrtle dies right after**
    A. meeting Daisy
    B. having sex with Gatsby
    C. arguing with her husband
    D. having sex with Tom

5. **What article does Gatz show Nick?**
    A. a purse
    B. a jacket
    C. a notebook
    D. a shoe

6. **Who first discuss car accidents?**
    A. Jordan and Tom
    B. Jordan and Nick
    C. Nick and Gatsby
    D. Daisy and Jordan

7. What concept does this novel undermine?
A. aestheticism
B. Bildungsroman genre
C. post–modernism
D. the American Dream

8. What phrase did Fitzgerald coin?
A. the Roaring Twenties
B. the Jazz Age
C. the Great War
D. Prohibition

9. What area did Fitzgerald spend the end of his life in?
A. East Egg
B. West Egg
C. the Riviera
D. the Midwest

10. Of what disease did Fitzgerald die?
A. cancer
B. heart disease
C. alcoholism
D. lung disease

11. Wilson shoots Gatsby and
A. Myrtle
B. himself
C. Tom
D. Daisy

12. After the murder, Tom and Daisy
A. go out of town
B. divorce
C. confess
D. seperate

13. When she sees Gatsby's shirts, Daisy
A. cries in despair
B. kisses him
C. calls her husband
D. cries for joy

14. From whom does Tom constantly recieve phone calls?
A. Myrtle
B. Catherine
C. Nick
D. Daisy

15. Catherine is
A. Daisy's sister
B. Gatsby's sister
C. Myrtle's sister
D. Tom's sister

16. The novel takes place in all but
A. East Egg
B. West Egg
C. the Midwest
D. New York City

17. Who in this novel does not have an affair?
A. Myrtle
B. Tom
C. Catherine
D. Daisy

18. Who arranges Gatsby and Daisy's reunion?
A. Gatsby
B. Tom
C. Nick
D. Daisy

19. **What does Gatsby offer in exchange for setting up this meeting?**
   A. a kickback
   B. a job
   C. a wife
   D. money

20. **Gatsby was born into the**
   A. European royalty
   B. lower–class
   C. elite
   D. noveau riche

21. **Gatsby fought in**
   A. the Vietnam War
   B. Congress
   C. WWI
   D. WWII

22. **How many children does Daisy have?**
   A. one
   B. two
   C. none
   D. three

23. **Before Daisy's arrival, Gatsby is**
   A. in a coma
   B. nervous
   C. collected
   D. hyperventilating

24. **The most common symbol of the dangers of wealth is**
   A. cities
   B. factories
   C. gold
   D. cars

25. What ultimately kills Gatsby are his
    A. morals
    B. criminal connections
    C. romantic commitments
    D. bootlegging scams

Quiz 4 Answer Key

1. **(A)** that she is engaged to someone else
2. **(A)** illegal activities
3. **(A)** he has found out that his wife is having an affair
4. **(C)** arguing with her husband
5. **(C)** a notebook
6. **(B)** Jordan and Nick
7. **(D)** the American Dream
8. **(B)** the Jazz Age
9. **(C)** the Riviera
10. **(C)** alcoholism
11. **(B)** himself
12. **(A)** go out of town
13. **(D)** cries for joy
14. **(A)** Myrtle
15. **(C)** Myrtle's sister
16. **(C)** the Midwest
17. **(C)** Catherine
18. **(C)** Nick
19. **(B)** a job
20. **(B)** lower–class
21. **(C)** WWI
22. **(A)** one
23. **(B)** nervous
24. **(D)** cars
25. **(C)** romantic commitments

ClassicNotes

GradeSaver™

Getting you the grade since 1999™

Other ClassicNotes from GradeSaver™

1984
Absalom, Absalom
Adam Bede
The Adventures of Augie
  March
The Adventures of
  Huckleberry Finn
The Adventures of Tom
  Sawyer
The Aeneid
Agamemnon
The Age of Innocence
Alice in Wonderland
All My Sons
All Quiet on the Western
  Front
All the King's Men
All the Pretty Horses
The Ambassadors
American Beauty
Angela's Ashes
Animal Farm
Anna Karenina
Antigone
Antony and Cleopatra
Aristotle's Ethics
Aristotle's Poetics
Aristotle's Politics
As I Lay Dying
As You Like It
The Awakening
Babbitt
The Bacchae
Bartleby the Scrivener
The Bean Trees
The Bell Jar

Beloved
Benito Cereno
Beowulf
Billy Budd
Black Boy
Bleak House
Bluest Eye
Brave New World
Breakfast at Tiffany's
Call of the Wild
Candide
The Canterbury Tales
Cat's Cradle
Catch-22
The Catcher in the Rye
The Caucasian Chalk
  Circle
The Cherry Orchard
The Chosen
A Christmas Carol
Chronicle of a Death
  Foretold
Civil Disobedience
Civilization and Its
  Discontents
A Clockwork Orange
The Color of Water
The Color Purple
Comedy of Errors
Communist Manifesto
A Confederacy of
  Dunces
Connecticut Yankee in
  King Arthur's Court
Coriolanus

The Count of Monte
  Cristo
Crime and Punishment
The Crucible
Cry, the Beloved
  Country
The Crying of Lot 49
Cymbeline
Daisy Miller
Death in Venice
Death of a Salesman
The Death of Ivan Ilych
Democracy in America
Devil in a Blue Dress
The Diary of Anne Frank
Disgrace
Divine Comedy-I:
  Inferno
A Doll's House
Don Quixote Book I
Don Quixote Book II
Dr. Faustus
Dr. Jekyll and Mr. Hyde
Dracula
Dubliners
East of Eden
Emma
Ender's Game
Endgame
Ethan Frome
The Eumenides
Everything is Illuminated
Fahrenheit 451
The Fall of the House of
  Usher
Farewell to Arms

For our full list of over 250 Study Guides, Quizzes,
Sample College Application Essays, Literature Essays and E-texts, visit:

www.gradesaver.com

ClassicNotes

GrAdeSaver™

Getting you the grade since 1999™

Other ClassicNotes from GradeSaver™

The Federalist Papers
For Whom the Bell Tolls
The Fountainhead
Frankenstein
Franny and Zooey
Glass Menagerie
The God of Small Things
The Grapes of Wrath
Great Expectations
The Great Gatsby
Hamlet
The Handmaid's Tale
Hard Times
Heart of Darkness
Hedda Gabler
Henry IV (Pirandello)
Henry IV Part 1
Henry IV Part 2
Henry V
The Hobbit
Homo Faber
House of Mirth
House of the Seven
   Gables
The House of the Spirits
House on Mango Street
Howards End
A Hunger Artist
I Know Why the Caged
   Bird Sings
An Ideal Husband
Iliad
The Importance of Being
   Earnest
In Our Time
Inherit the Wind

Invisible Man
The Island of Dr. Moreau
Jane Eyre
Jazz
The Joy Luck Club
Julius Caesar
Jungle of Cities
Kidnapped
King Lear
Last of the Mohicans
Leviathan
Libation Bearers
The Lion, the Witch and
   the Wardrobe
Lolita
Long Day's Journey Into
   Night
Lord Jim
Lord of the Flies
The Lord of the Rings:
   The Fellowship of the
   Ring
The Lord of the Rings:
   The Return of the
   King
The Lord of the Rings:
   The Two Towers
A Lost Lady
The Love Song of J.
   Alfred Prufrock
Lucy
Macbeth
Madame Bovary
Manhattan Transfer
Mansfield Park
MAUS

The Mayor of
   Casterbridge
Measure for Measure
Medea
Merchant of Venice
Metamorphoses
The Metamorphosis
Middlemarch
Midsummer Night's
   Dream
Moby Dick
Moll Flanders
Mother Courage and Her
   Children
Mrs. Dalloway
Much Ado About
   Nothing
My Antonia
Native Son
Night
No Exit
Notes from Underground
O Pioneers
The Odyssey
Oedipus Rex / Oedipus
   the King
Of Mice and Men
The Old Man and the Sea
On Liberty
One Day in the Life of
   Ivan Denisovich
One Flew Over the
   Cuckoo's Nest
One Hundred Years of
   Solitude
Oroonoko

For our full list of over 250 Study Guides, Quizzes,
Sample College Application Essays, Literature Essays and E-texts, visit:

www.gradesaver.com

ClassicNotes

GradeSaver™

Getting you the grade since 1999™

Other ClassicNotes from GradeSaver™

Othello
Our Town
Pale Fire
Paradise Lost
A Passage to India
The Pearl
The Picture of Dorian
    Gray
Poems of W.B. Yeats:
    The Rose
Portrait of the Artist as a
    Young Man
Pride and Prejudice
Prometheus Bound
Pudd'nhead Wilson
Pygmalion
Rabbit, Run
A Raisin in the Sun
The Real Life of
    Sebastian Knight
Red Badge of Courage
The Republic
Richard II
Richard III
The Rime of the Ancient
    Mariner
Robinson Crusoe
Roll of Thunder, Hear
    My Cry
Romeo and Juliet
A Room of One's Own
A Room With a View
Rosencrantz and
    Guildenstern Are
    Dead
Salome

The Scarlet Letter
Secret Sharer
Sense and Sensibility
A Separate Peace
Shakespeare's Sonnets
Siddhartha
Silas Marner
Sir Gawain and the
    Green Knight
Sister Carrie
Six Characters in Search
    of an Author
Slaughterhouse Five
Snow Falling on Cedars
The Social Contract
Something Wicked This
    Way Comes
Song of Roland
Sons and Lovers
The Sorrows of Young
    Werther
The Sound and the Fury
Spring Awakening
The Stranger
A Streetcar Named
    Desire
The Sun Also Rises
Tale of Two Cities
The Taming of the Shrew
The Tempest
Tender is the Night
Tess of the D'Urbervilles
Their Eyes Were
    Watching God
Things Fall Apart
The Threepenny Opera

The Time Machine
Titus Andronicus
To Build a Fire
To Kill a Mockingbird
To the Lighthouse
Treasure Island
Troilus and Cressida
Turn of the Screw
Twelfth Night
Ulysses
Uncle Tom's Cabin
Utopia
A Very Old Man With
    Enormous Wings
The Visit
Volpone
Waiting for Godot
Waiting for Lefty
Walden
Washington Square
Where the Red Fern
    Grows
White Fang
White Noise
White Teeth
Who's Afraid of Virginia
    Woolf
Winesburg, Ohio
The Winter's Tale
Woyzeck
Wuthering Heights
The Yellow Wallpaper
Yonnondio: From the
    Thirties

For our full list of over 250 Study Guides, Quizzes,
Sample College Application Essays, Literature Essays and E-texts, visit:

www.gradesaver.com

Made in the USA
Lexington, KY
11 August 2019